CW00725108

Sea Slug
Canada a
of Maine

by
J. Sherman Bleakney

Nimbus Publishing and
The Nova Scotia Museum
Halifax, Nova Scotia 1996

© Crown copyright, Nova Scotia, 1996

96 97 98 99 00   5 4 3 2 1

Produced as part of the Nova Scotia Museum Program
of the Department of Education and Culture, Province
of Nova Scotia

Minister: Honourable Robbie Harrison
Deputy Minister: Marilyn Gaudet

Co-published by the Nova Scotia Museum
and Nimbus Publishing Limited

A product of the Nova Scotia Government Co-Publishing Program

Illustrated by: Moira Cavanaugh and Twila Robar-DeCoste

Moira Cavanagh drew the illustrations on pp. 50, 59, 69, 75, 100, 130, 133,
155, and 158, which originally appeared in the *Keys to the Fauna and Flora of
Minas Basin.* (Wolfville, N.S.: Acadia University Institute), 1995.

Twila Robar-DeCoste modifed and redrew the illustrations on pp. 81,
84, 88, 110, 113, 121, 127, 140, 171, and 177 from drawings by Moira
Cavanagh, which originally appeared in the *Key to the Fauna and Flora
of Minas Basin* (Wolfville, N.S.: Acadia University Institute), 1995.*I*
Twila Robar-DeCoste drew the illustrations on pp. 24, 47, 53, 65, 75,
92, 95, 98, 103, 105, 108, 116, 118, 120, 124, 136, 143, 146, 149, 152, 167,
and 196 for this publication.

Edited by: Susan Lucy
Design/Cover photo: Ivan Murphy
Printed by: McCurdy Printing and Typesetting Limited

Produced by Communications Nova Scotia
and the Nova Scotia Museum

Canadian Cataloguing in Publication Data

Bleakney, J. Sherman (John Sherman)

Sea slugs of Atlantic Canada and the Gulf of Maine.
Co-published by the Nova Scotia Museum.
Includes bibliographical references and index.
ISBN 1-55109-192-5

1. Nudibranchiata—Atlantic Provinces. 2. Nudibranchiata—Maine,
Gulf of. I. Nova Scotia Museum. II. Title.

QL430.4.B53 1996   594.36   C96-950183-8

Table of Contents

Preface

BEAUTY FIT FOR A QUEEN

Sea slugs are beautiful, the very antithesis of garden slugs, so stop saying "yuk!" Unwrinkle your face, and read on. These marine creatures are so beautiful that it is said, and quite truthfully, that sea slugs are to the marine biologist what butterflies are to the entomologist or what orchids are to the botanist. In short, they are exquisite, flamboyant, extravagant—almost awesome.

Within the past decade, colour photographs of these highly photogenic marine animals have begun to appear on magazine covers and in nature calendars, and living specimens often are highlighted in natural history underwater documentaries. Entire international scientific conferences are devoted to research reports concerning sea slugs. Usually, one conference evening is set aside at which delegates gather just to show and share their best colour photos of these extravagant creatures.

Are you still unconvinced? Well, when Her Royal Highness, Queen Elizabeth, visited Scripps Institution of Oceanography in California in 1983, the institute's directors easily agreed upon an appropriate regal gift, one truly representing the world's oceans. They presented the royal couple with framed colour photographs of sea slugs. Thus, as a subtitle for this book, "Beauty Fit for a Queen" would not be an exaggeration! However, you need not be a queen, nor travel to California to discover the joys of sea slugs. There is a treasure trove right here in Atlantic Canada adequate to satisfy all your scientific and aesthetic cravings. For starters, there are the 47 species introduced in this book.

Acknowledgements

For the author, this little book is a personal celebration of an innate and insatiable curiosity about nature. That interest turned professional in 1950. In the summer of that year, the Nova Scotia Museum, under Director Donald Crowdis, engaged me to travel about the province in quest of amphibians and reptiles. That invaluable and formative experience led to a curatorship at the (then) National Museum of Canada, which led to a Ph.D., which in turn led to a professorship at Acadia University. For over 40 years, those three institutions have provided the financial and physical resources and the vital intellectual freedom for me and my students to enjoy the challenges and the rewards of investigating nature. Their substantial support, both direct and indirect, is sincerely acknowledged.

For many years the (then) National Research Council of Canada provided funding for my research in Atlantic Canada and for studies in Europe and on Pacific Ocean shores. In 1967–68, under the superb tutelage of Dr. T. E. Thompson, Bristol University, and of Dr. Henning Lemche, University Zoology Museum, Copenhagen, I became inescapably a sea slug specialist. Sadly, neither gentleman has lived to see this fruition of their initial influence. Their past encouragements are gratefully acknowledged. Several copyright illustrations in this book are reproduced through permission of The Ray Society (T. E. Thompson, 1976, *Biology of Opisthobranch Molluscs*, Vol. I: fig. 2, g; fig. 7, a; fig. 8, a), Ophelia Publications

(H. Just and M. Edmunds, 1985, *North Atlantic Nudibranchs seen by Henning Lemche,* Plate 26B), and McGraw-Hill Inc. (L. H. Hyman, 1967, *The Invertebrates*, Vol. VI, Mollusca, fig. 162, G; fig. 163, C and G; fig. 164, A; and fig. 217 in part). The bulk of the black and white drawings are originals and were generated from my personal collection of colour transparencies, and from a few figures in Alder and Hancock's 1845–55 monograph. In 1979–80, Moira Cavanagh produced a set of 24 drawings for my *Key to the Fauna and Flora of Minas Basin.* Nine of those originals are included in this book. Ten others from that set were modified and redrawn by Twila Robar-DeCoste, who herself added another 19 new drawings to the collection. The illustrative talents of these two biology graduates are acknowledged with considerable envy.

Additional thank-yous are due to typist and naturalist Lana Ashby who somehow translated and transcribed my handwriting onto an equally incomprehensible microdisk. Processing of the draft manuscript through the Nova Scotia Museum publication channels has been guided by Mr. John Hennigar-Shuh, Mr. Fred Scott, and Dr. Derek Davis. Valuable editorial input has been provided by Barbara R. Robertson, Susan Walker, but most especially by Susan Lucy, Coordinator Editorial Services, Communications Nova Scotia.

Last, but foremost, an acknowledgement for my wife, Nancy, an unofficial and unsalaried field assistant since 1952. Our marriage began with five-month long herpetological honeymoon in eastern Canada collecting slimy frogs and salamanders. Some 30 years later our second honeymoon in 1981 was a 10-month safari around the Pacific collecting slimy sea slugs. Of such are the sacrifices of the wives of scientists, and the true meaning of spousal support beyond the call of duty.

How to Use This Book

This book has a decidedly dual purpose: to serve both the scientific community and the general public. For professional biologists, the data, the illustrations, and the references—a distillate of information accumulated over the past 30 years—will provide a comprehensive guide to an important but neglected group of marine animals in Atlantic Canada.

But this is also a book that the marine professional can easily recommend to nonprofessional friends and to those conservationists unaware of the intrinsic values of opisthobranchs. Much of the text material is written for nonspecialist readers such as teachers, students, and amateur naturalists; and a detailed, illustrated glossary is included to explain the scientific terms used in the text—from aeolid to zooplankton. To make it easier to find, the page margins of the glossary are shaded.

Because some readers will want to see these creatures in the flesh, the book can be used as a field guide. Hints on collecting, preserving, and identifying sea slugs and a pictorial key are located near the front of the book, and the margins of the pictorial key pages are shaded for quick reference. Detailed accounts of individual species follow.

To use the book as a field guide, you must first catch your slug. Then turn to the Beginner's Pictorial Key to Sea Slugs on page 37 and match up your specimen with one of the 23 genera shown there. The slugs shown in the key are grouped according to where they can be found, and that information and general body shape can usually provide an answer in 60 seconds or less.

When you have matched your specimen as closely as possible to one in the pictorial key, turn to the page indicated. There among the species accounts you may find additional drawings and descriptions. For example, Figures 4 and 5 detail five species of *Coryphella* and their tiny teeth. It is only through a four-year Ph.D. study by A. M. Kuzirian in the 1970s that we now know how to tell these species apart.

But you don't have to get your feet wet to enjoy these fascinating creatures. To learn more about sea slugs in general, start by reading the section entitled Introducing—The Sea Slug, starting on page 19, which discusses their origins, their biology, and the frequently asked question "What are they good for?" For more detail, go on to the Species Accounts: Descriptions and Comments for separate text descriptions of 42 species (although in total 47 species are discussed). Each includes a black and white illustration, that species' classification and scientific name, a brief anatomical description, notes on natural history, known distribution, and a comments section in which unusual aspects will be highlighted. The nonspecialist is particularly encouraged to read the comments section. There you will encounter the intellectual excitement of challenge and discovery that motivates the research biologist. Hopefully, this text may lead a few young readers to choose such a career, while other readers may simply appreciate having their awareness of nature expanded to include these beautiful molluscs.

If you want to learn more, there are many interesting articles to read, and they are listed in species sequence in the section References for Particular Species and in four other reference sections:

Note that the same species sequence is employed in the Table of Contents, in the Pictorial Key in the Species Accounts, in the References for Particular Species, and in the Annotated Classification Scheme for Sea Slugs. It couldn't be made any easier!

A Note on Names

Unlike most birds, mammals, and fish, these opisthobranchs have no established common names. Several authors (Abbott, 1974; Gosner, 1979) provided their own names, but their personal choices unfortunately differ. In 1988, the first international attempt at standardization of molluscan vernacular names appeared in the American Fisheries Society Special Publication No. 16 (Turgeon, 1988). However, less than half of sacoglossans (herbivorous sea slugs) and nudibranchs (carnivorous species) were provided with names, and many of those are either uninformative or inappropriate. Obviously, this sea slug branch of molluscan biology is still in its unstable infancy. There is, therefore, no excuse for not learning the scientific names. Actually, this can be an edifying and entertaining experience as explained in the next section entitled The Joy of Scientific Terminology.

With species and genera still flipping back and forth, and with some Atlantic and Pacific species being united into one species, it seems inappropriate to try to keep up the same pace with a set of common names. For these reasons, the species in this text are referred to only by their scientific generic or specific names. In species where long-standing names have recently been changed, the older equivalent name has been added within brackets and preceded by an equals symbol.

To delve more deeply into the subject of scientific names and classification, turn to the two sections Annotated Classification Scheme for Sea Slugs and Classification List of Atlantic Canada and Gulf of Maine Opisthobranchs at the back of this book.

The Joy of Scientific Terminology

If you ever expect to become a scientist and enjoy it, you must learn the language. Those tongue twisters of scientific terminology are derived for the most part from Greek and Latin, but so, also, is much of our English language. Thus, the more scientific terms you dissect, the more you begin to appreciate the true meaning of our everyday language, and your personal vocabulary grows in depth and breadth.

To get to the root of the language of science, you must have an old or new edition of that fascinating book *A Source Book of Biological Names and Terms* by Edmund C. Jaeger, which was first published in 1944, was last revised in 1978, and is still in print. (You will find its complete reference under References—General in this book.) Then, curl up in a comfy chair, and get ready for some intellectual excitement in a far-out dimension as you translate Greek and Latin scientific names from your favourite biology field guides.

For example, look up the bird blue jay. You may not realize it, but every plant and animal species has a unique, internationally accepted scientific name, which is usually and traditionally an attempt to sketch its diagnostic features in Greek and/or Latin. Blue jays are known the world over to all scientists as *Cyanocitta cristata*. What does *that* mean? If it's all Greek to you, consult Mr. Jaeger and find that *cyan* = blue; *citta* = chatter or screech; *crist* = crested. *Voilà!* We have a translation that reads "a crested, blue screecher." The common song sparrow's scientific name is *Melospiza melodia*. Since *melo* = song; *spiza* = finch; and *melodia* = pleasantly singing or melodious, then our little sparrow is aptly described as "a songster finch that is particularly melodious."

This translation approach, I think you will agree, provides substantial motivation for the requisite memoriziation of scientific names. It becomes a word game, and some words may even elicit a chuckle. There is a hydroid group, preyed upon by sea slugs, with the improbably generic designation of *Zyzzyzus*. This is honest Latin for "double zigzag."

The following is a sampling of translations of sea slug scientific names. Note that this terminology is not limited to anatomy, since people, places, and even Greek gods are quite acceptable. A few sea slug field guides have made up common names simply by translating the Greek and Latin terminology. Thus, *Dendronotus frondosus* becomes the Bushy-backed Nudibranch, because *dendr* = treelike; *not* = back; and *frond* = leafy.

acanth *(G)*	thorns, spiny
Aeolidia *(G)*	diminutive of Aeolis, Greek god of wind
Alderia	after Joshua Alder, sea slug pioneer of the 1850s
bostoniensis	after Boston, Mass.
cera *(G)*	horn, horned
concinna *(L)*	skilfully joined, neat
coronata *(L)*	crowned, with coronet
dendro *(G)*	tree, branching
exiguus *(L)*	tiny, short
frondosus *(L)*	bushy, leafy
gibbosa *(L)*	hunched, humped
gracilis *(L)*	slender
gymnota *(G)*	naked
laevis *(L)*	smooth
muricata *(L)*	full of sharp points
nana *(G)*	dwarf
nodosa *(L)*	knotty, knobby
onchi *(G)*	with tubercules
pilosa *(L)*	hairy, hairlike
poly *(G)*	many
verrucosa *(L)*	warty
viridis *(L)*	green

Some Useful Terms

A GLOSSARY

Aeolid   That spectacular subgroup of **nudibranchs** having finger-like **cerata** on the **dorsum**.

Arborescent   Repeatedly branched, tree-like; as in certain types of gills and **cerata**.

Ascoglossa   That distinct group of sea slugs that suck the cell sap from seaweeds, logically referred to as algal sap suckers. As the teeth they use to cut through plant cell walls gradually wear, they are replaced by new teeth, and the worn ones are shed from the tongue and stored in a little sac beneath the tongue. Greek for bag = *asc* and for tongue = *gloss*. Historically, this name and **sacoglossa** have been used interchangeably.

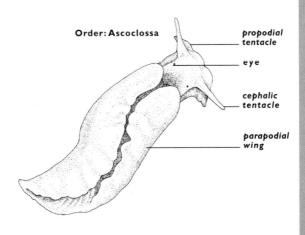

Order: Ascoclossa

propodial tentacle
eye
cephalic tentacle
parapodial wing

Benthic   Living on the floor of the ocean, whether in shallow or deep water. Benthic creatures may burrow, crawl, or attach.

Bryozoa   Tiny, colonial animals that usually reproduce by budding and forming encrusting, branching, or mosslike (*bryo* = moss) colonies permanently attached on stones, wharves, and such. Also known as **Ectoprocta.**

Buccal   Referring to the mouth region or mouth cavity.

Calcareous   Objects containing calcium carbonate, the stuff of chalk and limestone and snail shells.

Ceras   Singular form of cerata.

Cerata (pl.)   Finger-like projections on the backs of sea slugs; they may be single or in clusters and often contain branches of the digestive tract, respiratory blood vessels, poison glands, and sacs of stinging cells taken from their **Cnidarian** prey.

Chitinous   Having chitin as a component; an extremely tough and flexible complex of chemicals found in the shells of crustaceans, the skins of insects, and the **perisarc** of **hydroids.**

Chloroplasts   Plant **organelles** that contain the chlorophyll of photosynthesis. It is these microscopic structures that many **sacoglossan** sea slugs can incorporate and accommodate in their own tissues as **kleptoplasts.**

Cnidaria　　A major group of animals, including jellyfish, hydroids, corals, and sea anemones, all of which possess stinging cells **(cnidoblasts)**.

Cnidoblasts　Unique to **Cnidarian** animals, cells that contain a special capsule **(nematocyst)** capable of shooting out a hypodermic thread **(nematosome)** that can penetrate skin and inject poisons as lethal as cobra venom.

Cnidosac　　Chamber near the tip of each **ceras** in the **aeolid nudibranch** slugs that houses hundreds of **nematocysts** taken from **Cnidarian** prey. This muscular chamber has a pore and can eject swarms of nematocysts as a means of defence.

Coenosarc　　Soft inner body tissues of a **hydroid,** protected by a tough outer **chitinous** skin, the **perisarc.**

Suborder: Doridacea

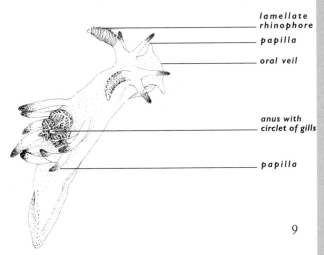

lamellate rhinophore

papilla

oral veil

anus with circlet of gills

papilla

9

Comb jelly   Planktonic jelly balls and jelly cylinders, but without the stinging cells of true jellyfish. They swim by means of eight rows of hundreds of paddle-like combs that are so unique that these animals constitute a distinct phylum, the Ctenophora (*cten* = comb; *phora* = bearers).

Copepods   Teeming, minute, chiefly free-swimming crustaceans that are important as fish food. Their abundance in the world's oceans is of such magnitude that ecologically they are justifiably referred to as "the insects of the sea."

Crinoids   Related to and resembling starfish, but most are attached by a long stalk and do not crawl about.

Dorid   Slug group having a circle of gills on the back with the anus at the centre. (Kind of shakes one's faith in natural selection.)

Suborder: Doridacea

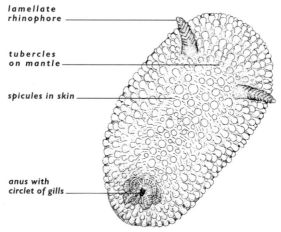

lamellate
rhinophore

tubercles
on mantle

spicules in skin

anus with
circlet of gills

Dorsum   The upper surface of an animal; for molluscs the terms **notum** and **mantle** refer to the same area. Hence **dorsal**, or on, or near the back.

Ectoprocta   Another officially acceptable name for the phylum **Bryozoa**.

Epizoitic   Living upon the surface of an animal, either physically attached or just hanging out with; in other words, never parasitic.

Fathom   Measure equivalent to 1.8 m (6 ft.), chiefly used in measuring water depth.

Genera   Plural of **genus.**

Genus   Group name for animal or plant species having common structural characteristics distinct from those of any other species groups.

Gonad   A reproductive organ capable of producing eggs or sperm, or both.

Gymnosome   Literally "naked body,"(*gymno* = naked; *soma* = body). That group of pelagic sea slugs that lack shells and have to swim in their birthday suits.

Hermaph-roditic   Possessing the reproductive organs of both sexes and producing both eggs and sperm, as do all sea slugs. In contrast, the common shelled sea snails of our shores are either male or female.

Hydroid   Major division of the stinging phylum **Cnidaria** and a favourite food of aeolid nudibranchs; tend to form bushy plant-like colonies tipped with hundreds of little flower-like tentacled animals loaded with stinging cells. Fire coral is one form and is so named not because of its colour but because that is how it feels when you touch it.

Intertidal The extent of air-exposed seashore from the upper-most storm salt-spray zone to the lowest of the low tides. It can be subdivided into many zones based on physical, botanical, and zoological criteria.

Irruptive Marked, sudden increase in the relative numbers of a natural population, and usually associated with favourable alteration of the environment such as unlimited food.

Kleptoplasts **Chloroplasts** stolen from plants and used by **sacoglossan** molluscs to make mucus (*klepto* = to steal, as in kleptomaniac).

Suborder: Dendronotacea

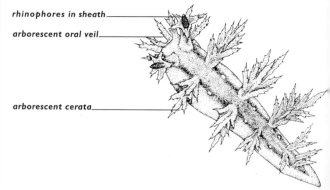

rhinophores in sheath

arborescent oral veil

arborescent cerata

Krill Planktonic shrimp-type crustaceans that constitute the principal food of certain whales.

Lamellate **Tentacles** with layers and layers of circular shelving resembling a stack of plates, or a Japanese pagoda, depending upon your aesthetic perspicacity.

Lecithotrophic Literally "yolk-food" (*lecith* = yolk; *troph* = food), a term applied to newly hatched larvae that live off their yolk reserves for days and days and thus do not have to hunt for food. *See* **planktotrophic.**

Malacologist Someone who specializes in the study of molluscs, a group of 80,000 species that includes chitons, snails, clams, squids, and octopuses. What they all have in common is a soft body (very edible), which may or may not sit in a shell. The root word for soft in Greek is *malac-*, and the Latin is *moll-*. (Perhaps malacologists don't study malacuscs because they can't pronounce the word!)

Mantle The slimy skin covering the back of a mollusc. Besides mucus, it has the organizational ability to secrete a beautiful shell or a spiny spicule-filled skin or clusters of soft, waving stinging cerata.

Morphology Refers to the shape of something, be it the shape of the whole animal or only one of its parts.

Nematocyst Literally "thread-cyst," the stinging weapon of jellyfish and their kin.

Notum The **dorsal** surfaces, in particular any dorso-lateral ridge upon which **cerata** are positioned. Hence **notal** ridge.

Operculum **Calcareous** or **chitinous** door that covers the opening when snails withdraw into their shell; present only in the larval stages of sea slugs.

Opisthobranch Literally "rear-gills" (*opisth* = towards the rear; *branch* = gill structure) and refers to sea slugs in general, because their gills are not at the front (proso-branch) as is typical of shelled marine snails.

Oral hood Also referred to as the oral "veil," a fleshy extension of the head out over the mouth. May be simple or fringed with **arborescent papillae.**

Oral tentacle **Tentacle** adjacent to the mouth, and undoubtedly a chemosensory food tester.

Organelles Microscopically detectable structures within cells that perform special functions; these functions acting in concert create and maintain our daily lives.

Papillae Finger-like extensions with diameter much smaller than length, their surface may be smooth or rough.

Parapodial Fleshy side extensions of the body, often used for swimming but in the **genus** *Elysia* they serve mainly as a respiratory surface.

Pelagic A laid-back life style of drifting with ocean currents and sea winds; no crawling on muddy bottoms and no roughing it on rocky shores.

Perisarc Hard, chitinous, plastic-like covering on many hydroids. *See* **Coenosarc**.

Pheromones Sort of aerosol behavioural hormones, extensively employed by invertebrates for organizing family affairs, love affairs, and warfares.

Plankton Tiny plants (**phytoplankton**) and animals (**zooplankton**) that drift about in the ocean, usually in concentrated swarms that attract sea birds, whales, and sea slugs.

Planktotrophic Term applied to newly hatched larvae with no yolk, which must eat plankton to survive (*see* **lecithotrophic**).

Propodial Tentacles at the front corners of the broad ventral foot of snails.

Pteropods Literally "wing-footed" (*pter* = wing; *pod* = foot) refers to those pelagic slugs with parapodial flaps used in swimming.

Suborder: Aeolidacea

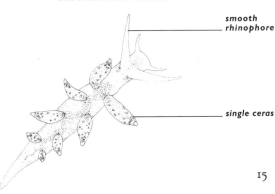

smooth rhinophore

single ceras

Radula　Unique to molluscs, a mobile rasping tongue made up of rows and rows of hard teeth mounted on a tough conveyer belt called the radular ribbon. This very versatile structure can be used for drilling holes, shredding, puncturing, spearing, and scraping.

Rhinophore　A special pair of **tentacles**, whose shape and colours can be very elaborate, located on top of the heads of sea slugs, and loaded with mysterious sensory structures.

Sacoglossa　Same as **ascoglossa**, the algal sap-sucking sea slugs, but with a Latin twist using the Roman root *sac-* for the storage sack portion of the term. This is the term currently in vogue at pre-symposia cocktail parties.

Sessile　Plant or animal that is firmly attached, by some means, to the sea bottom.

Speciation　That process of evolutionary natural selection by which individual variations broaden population diversity, and components of that diversity become separated and more anatomically specialized. These variations eventually become genetically incompatible with the parent species, and thereby initiate a new **species**.

Species　Group subordinate in classification to **genus** having members of common ancestry that interbreed and differ only in minor details.

Spicules	Hard crystalline rods in the skins of many **dorid nudibranchs**, which can be densely interwoven to produce a firm and spiny **mantle**. Certain **tubercles** may be packed with spicules.
Stolon	Horizontal, rootlike outgrowth, branched or unbranched, common to many colonial animals, including **hydroids**, from which new buds form new colonies.
Tentacle	A term applied to paired sensory projections in the head region; sort of extra-specialized **papillae.**
Tentaculiform	In the shape/form of tentacles.
Thecosome	Literally "encased-body," refers to those **pelagic** sea slugs that possess a shell—but for what purpose? The **Gymnosomes** eat nothing else and do it by simply pulling the Thecs right out of their shells.

Suborder: Aeolidacea

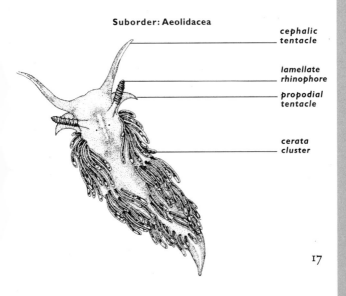

cephalic tentacle

lamellate rhinophore

propodial tentacle

cerata cluster

Tripinnate   Triple-branching pattern of some gills, wherein the central shaft has side branches, and these in turn have side branches.

Tubercle   Small elevation with base wider than height; can be smooth, warty, and even spiny with **spicules**.

Tunicate   Common marine animals, mostly sessile, encased in a tough cellulose tunic (sac). Yes, animal cellulose, and the tunic has valuable antibiotic properties as well!

Veliger   Little planktonic mulluscan larva possessing a spiral shell. These hatch from many species of sea slug eggs, but the shell is shed when the larva bottoms-out after its peripatetic plankton phase.

Ventral   On the underside, opposite of **dorsal**.

Vernacular   The local common name for something, often misleading and unscientific but rather colourful: "blood sucker" for jellyfish, "darning needle" for dragonfly, "lizard" for salamander, and "yuk" for slug.

Zooplankton   Animal life of the **plankton**; includes many kinds of eggs, larval stages, and small adults, with **copepods** dominant.

Introducing—
The Sea Slug

WHAT IS A SEA SLUG?

It is unfortunate that sea slugs have to be saddled with the same disgusting name as those horrid garden pests. The term slug is about all that they share, as the two groups have had quite a different evolutionary history, which is reflected in their anatomy and ecology. Both are, of course, true molluscan snails of the class Gastropoda. However, whereas garden slugs are "repulsive agricultural pests," nearly every kind of sea slug can be considered "a thing of beauty, and a joy forever."

Backyard garden slugs are terrestrial; they evolved from land snails and as one might guess, they have lungs (not aquatic gills), large eyes (on the tip of their second pair of tentacles), and large yolky eggs (without aquatic larval stages). In contrast, sea slugs are exclusively marine; they evolved from an offshoot of marine snails whose initial evolutionary phase was spent ploughing and burrowing through silts, sands, and muds. This unusual burrowing lifestyle led to an elongated bilateral body symmetry (an uncoiling of the typical snail body), and all projections and other potential hangups were consequently reduced or lost, including the coiled external shell and lid (operculum), original gills, original tentacles, and large eyes, which were of little importance underground. It was probably this loss of the standard protective snail shell that initiated the development of chemical defence strategies, including the utilization of

FIG. I *Diversity of Sea Slug Body Forms*

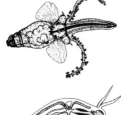

Order: Gymnosomata-*Crucibranchaea*
Planktonic, shell-less, carnivore with swimming wings and sucker-equipped tentacles

Suborder: Dendronotacea-*Phylliroe*
Planktonic, fish-tailed, foot-less, predator of jellyfish

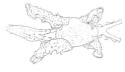

Order: Ascoglossa-*Lobiger*
Univalved herbivore with four parapodial extensions

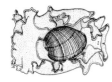

Order: Bullomorpha-*Hydatina*
Sand dweller, thin globose shell, expanded foot skirt

Order: Thecosomata-*Limacina*
Planktonic, shelled "butterfly," feeds on phytoplankton

Suborder: Dendronotacea-*Melibe*
Expanded head scoops up schools of copepods

Order: Ascoglossa-*Julia*
Bivalved herbivore with green shell and body

defensive toxins generated by other organisms. One restless evolutionary branch of this new shell-less, nearly blind, tentacle-less snail then returned to the surface of the silts and from there diversified and became adapted to most other marine habitats, including the open ocean, never to crawl again.

In doing so they experimented chromatically and morphologically, and it was this evolutionary flowering of drab mud-burrowers that produced today's splendid assemblage of nearly 3,000 species of sea slugs. So, the varied colours and colour patterns, the diverse shapes and textures of the mantle covering, the unusual foot and head forms, the delicate tentacles, gills, and papillae—all are newly evolved and unknown and unimaginable in any other molluscan group. Some of this diversity in body form is presented in Figure 1, with comments on function. One exotic species, appropriately named Spanish Dancer, swims short distances by undulating the folds of its red skirt: a difficult act for your average garden slug to follow.

THEIR BIOLOGY IN GENERAL

Much of what we believe we know about the biology of Atlantic Canada's opisthobranchs has been extrapolated from reports and studies done on the same or related species from the eastern United States or western Europe. Such information may not be altogether true for our area because our coastal environment differs from areas to the south and from European shores. The diversity of marine environments in Atlantic Canada is really quite astounding: the cold Labrador Current of east coast Newfoundland, the fertile Grand Banks, the Gulf of St. Lawrence system, the indented Atlantic coast of Nova Scotia, and the tide-swept Bay of Fundy. Add to this our two inland seas, the deep Bras d'Or Lake of Cape Breton Island with the world's least tides and the shallow Minas Basin with the world's largest tides. The influence of this spectrum of physical factors is immediately evident in the conspicuous differences in the marine algal communities of each area (Novaczak and McLachlan, 1988). Consequently, within this broad range of environmental combinations sea slugs from Canadian populations may, for example, be larger, live longer, lay more eggs, have a different larval history, eat different prey, appear at a different time of the year, or even be more poisonous than individuals of the same species collected from southern England or southern New England. It will be many, many years before ardent slug watchers and researchers will have gathered sufficient information to enable biologists to say when and where a particular nudibranch or sacoglossan species may be found, how many eggs it produces, what it eats and how much, and how important it is to the local ecosystem. Every imaginable marine ecosystem is involved, from tidal marshes and coastal waters to open ocean and abyssal depths. Amateur naturalists could contribute, as they have done historically in so many other natural history disciplines, by gathering much of this vital basic information. Such information is the backbone of conservation measures.

The individuals of many species of sea slugs live for but a few months, while others are regular annuals. Only the giant sea slugs, such as *Aplysia*, live for several years. These two life history patterns are associated with two major types of feeding strategies. Sea slugs that feed upon plant or animal prey that is abundant throughout the year tend to have a steady, stable life-style; they feed and grow and spawn once over a period of a year. Of necessity, slugs that feed upon prey species that have irruptive (marked by sudden sharp increases in their numbers) and short-lived growth patterns also

appear sporadically and have patchy distributions. They may complete their life history cycle in a matter of weeks or months. Their larvae locate and then settle on a hydroid colony, feed voraciously, grow and spawn on the hydroids, and continue feeding until all of that prey colony is consumed. At this point the adult slugs die of starvation, their eggs hatch, and the larvae drift away in hopes of finding other hydroid colonies. Because these slugs so often eliminate their food patch, they serve an important function in partially controlling what are termed "fouling organisms"—species of sponges, hydroids, bryozoans, sea anemones, and tunicates that appear seasonally to foul the hulls of boats, floating docks, and buoy markers. Note that these sites are some of the best and easiest from which to collect nudibranchs and sacoglossans.

Because individual sea slugs are both male and female and produce sperm and eggs at the same time, their "breeding" behaviour is a matter of a mutual exchange of sperm. There is usually a relatively large penis structure to facilitate sperm transfer, and there is usually a special target area on the right side of each slug behind which is a storage sac for sperm. The qualification "usually" is used because there are species, such as Alderia modesta, which are equipped with a needle-tipped, hypodermic penis. This they proceed to jab into any area of another individual's body, be it head, foot, or

FIG.2 *Examples of Egg Spawn Shapes*

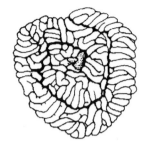

Aeolidia papillosa

Facelina bostoniensis

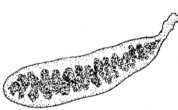

Alderia modesta

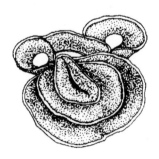

Onchidoris bilamellata

stomach. Somehow the injected sperm find their way to the ovary area.

Fertilized eggs are laid in strings surrounded by gelatinous layers, these strings are arranged in patterns within another gelatinous envelope, and this in turn is cemented to a substrate in species-distinct patterns of curves, coils, spirals, cloverleafs, cushions, and the like (Fig. 2). The patterns and colours of these egg masses form lovely complex designs and are a worthy challenge for the naturalist macrophotographer.

From the eggs may hatch miniature slugs (termed direct development) or swimming planktonic larvae (veligers). This fundamental difference is usually a genetically determined either/or situation for each species of slug. However, there are a few species with the unusual ability to switch from one type of egg production to the other in response to seasonal temperatures or fluctuations in food supply.

It is at these larval stages that mortality from predators is highest, for once the slugs begin feeding upon their usual prey, they become enveloped within a superb biochemical armour. Elementary deduction proves it: larval and juvenile sea slugs must be nothing less than delicious. Consider that some species of sea hares (*Aplysia*) lay nearly 1 million eggs per egg string and may produce over 400 million eggs in a few months. As only two of those larvae need survive to replace their parents, and as the ocean is not shore-to-shore sea hares, then 399,999,998 potential sea hares must have passed over the smiling lips of swarms of zooplankton and larval fish. The next time you eat seafood, just remember that your meal probably would not have survived to legal size without numerous banquets of sea slug larvae. Perhaps 30% of delicious scallop muscle is actually sea slug molecules!

WHAT ARE THEY GOOD FOR?

Having established their unrivaled aesthetic credibility, let us examine the other side of the coin and ask that direct question "What are they good for?" They are certainly not good to eat, being too small, too poisonous, or both, but they are good for the environment. If they did not fit into the scheme of life, if they were not one of the functional cogs, their extinction would have been visited upon their slimy selves long ago.

Although it seems unlikely, sea slugs are proving to be of direct benefit to humans as important organisms for investigating learning and behaviour, tissue transplant responses, and suppression of cancer, viruses, and bacteria. Because of the exceptionally large size and natural colour coding of certain cells in their brains, sea slugs of the genera *Aplysia*, *Tritonia*, and *Hermissenda* are ideal animals in which to study innate behaviour (instinct) as well as learned behaviour at the molecular level. During the 1980s scientists studying sea slugs were able, for the first time, to identify discrete compounds that are responsible for specific but nevertheless complex behaviour patterns. Even more exciting is the discovery and description of the chemical changes and adjustments that take place in nerve cells in the brain during a learning experience, as well as clues as to how that information is accessed when the animal needs to remember. These biochemical discoveries are directly applicable to brain nerve cells of all animals including humans. Understanding these molecules of memory is basic to eventually understanding the storage and retrieval mechanisms of our own brains. This information may someday help explain why those Canadians who ate toxic mussels from Prince Edward Island in 1987 had their most recent memories entirely erased.

There are two genera of sea slugs, *Aplysia* and *Tritonia,* that have been the subject of neurological research for 30 years in Europe and North America. These are large slugs, 15 to 30 cm in length, and they possess especially large nerve fibres, which are ideal for studying the conduction of information signals along nerves. A West Coast neurophysiologist once told me that during his high school years he earned spending money with his scuba gear by collecting slugs for research labs at rates of $5 to $10 per animal. So many of these valuable sea slugs have been collected along the coast of California by physiologists that they are now rather rare and perhaps endangered. One consequence is that stocks in Canada are coming under pressure and should now be included in conservation discussions. Another consequence, but a positive one, has been research efforts directed towards developing captive rearing methods for these species and thereby to supply the research community from these stocks, as is done in the case of laboratory mice.

Sea slugs eat the most dreadful food: sponges, jellyfish, sea anemones, corals, tunicates, tube worms, barnacles, and noxious seaweeds. These eating habits have led to some astounding situations, which are the subject of much medical research. Most of those food items are poisonous, loaded with chemical toxins, because, being soft, helpless, sessile creatures without tooth or fang or legs, their only feasible defence against all those hungry mouths in the ocean is chemical warfare. Their toxins help keep such predators as crabs and fish at bay, but our science fiction sea slugs voraciously consume these poisonous animals and plants, digest the good stuff, and then extract and somehow transfer the various poisons to their own skins for their own defence against hungry predators. Scientists would love to know how sea slugs block the intended effects of these poisons, how they store the toxins, and how they later release them.

Sea slugs that eat poisonous jellyfish, sea anemones, and hydroids have developed a truly fantastic technique that baffles biologists. Such prey are members of the phylum Cnidaria and are endowed with stinging cells that shoot out hollow hypodermic threads (nematocysts) that penetrate skin and then pump in poisons that are similar to cobra snake neurotoxins. The cnidarian upon which a sea slug is chewing may have as many as seven different types of stinging cells (cnidoblasts), but somehow the slug's stomach selects and sets aside the largest and most deadly coiled stinging threads for its own use and then disposes of the other six types by digesting them. The intact nematocysts, which are mysteriously numbed so that they do not shoot out their deadly threads, are then moved into special muscular storage sacs (cnidosacs) in the skin of the slug. If the slug is nibbled by a fish, the sacs squeeze out a batch of coiled poisonous threads, which now fire off their hypodermic weapons in all directions, and the fish learns something unforgettable about soft, defenceless-looking sea slugs.

Researchers working in the field of tissue transplants and organ transplants are somewhat envious of the abilities of sea slugs. Not only are there slugs that accept and maintain cells and organelles (discrete structures within cells) from other animal phyla, there are within one special group, the Sacoglossa, animals that specialize in sucking the sap out of marine algae. Several genera of these sap suckers can incorporate functional chlorophyll (the algal chloroplast organelles) into their own cells and quite literally turn themselves into plants. Incredibly, these slugs can keep the chloroplasts functioning for months, and the sugars produced by the plant component are then turned into useful mucus by the slug. Because these specialist slugs can actually take up both oxygen and carbon dioxide and can release both oxygen and carbon dioxide, they are a true animal/plant chimera. We marine biologists refer to them poetically as "leaves that crawl."

We have one such species in Atlantic Canada, *Elysia chlorotica*, that is quite famous in knowledgeable circles, such as the National Research Council (NRC) laboratories in Halifax. The usual habitat of this photosynthetic green sacoglossan is tidal marshes, where in summer it can be found basking in shallow water or even in air on the mud flats. If you ask three obvious questions about life on a marsh for a photosynthesizing slug, you get three fascinating answers. The questions are how do these little, soft, slimy things protect themselves (1) from predators, (2) from lethal ultraviolet wave lengths, and (3) from bacteria? First, the algae they feed upon are themselves toxic, and, as you could guess by now, so are the slugs. They simply (well, not so simply, really) add the algal toxins to their own concoctions, and thereby their skin becomes a veritable minefield of noxious glands. If the slugs are dropped into a fish tank, they are instantly gobbled up and instantaneously (that is the visual impression) spat out, after which the slugs crawl about the fish tank with impunity. Second, to protect their own cells, and in particular the delicate chloroplasts that they stole from the algae (and therefore referred to by some specialists as "kleptoplasts," meaning "stolen plastids"), they can generate on demand very special chemicals that absorb the deadly ultraviolet wavelengths. (If humans had this ability, it would mean no more sunburns nor skin cancer.) Scientists at NRC, Halifax, discovered that our local *Elysia chlorotica* has two such compounds, one of which, a polypropionate, was new to chemists. It was named elysione. The other UV-screening compound had been reported previously but from far away; it occurs in the skin of a sea slug living in coastal shallows of the Hawaiian Islands. Third, bacteria just love moist nutritious skin, as everyone knows who has cut their skin down to the wet stuff and got an "infected cut" from those ever-present bacteria. So to stave off armies of bacteria, slugs must produce antibiotics (as do fish, amphibians, and other slimy, moist-skinned creatures), and the NRC chemists determined that one of the antibiotics produced by *Elysia chlorotica* is an erythromycin compound, similar to the one that pharmaceutical companies routinely extract from the bacterial mould *Streptomyces*.

It is these protective compounds, produced in abundance by many sessile and delicate marine plants and animals, that greatly interest the pharmaceutical industry and the medical profession. Private companies often invest heavily in marine research facilities, usually in the subtropics or tropics. However, NRC, Halifax, has proven that northern latitudes have potential as well. Their labs have recently tested many local organisms and identified different compounds possessing activities such as antiviral, antibacterial, antifungal, cytolytic, and special anticancer properties, all obviously of potential medical benefit. Several of these newly discovered Atlantic Canada chemicals are being patented. Chemists at the University of Hawaii have recently identified additional sea slug chemicals that fall into the categories of insecticide, antileucemic, and cancer inducing (Scheuer, 1990)!

We could go on, but perhaps I have made my point, and you are now beginning to understand that when one speaks of sea slugs one speaks always in superlatives. Although neither "sea slug" nor "nudibranch" nor "sacoglossan" is as yet a household word, it won't be long now.

How to Find and Identify Sea Slugs

COLLECTING

Sacoglossans and nudibranchs may be found from the highest tidal levels to great depths off shore. Some very accessible habitats are tidal marshes and their creeks and pools; on and under intertidal rocks and seaweeds; in tide pools; in sea caves; on wharf pilings; and on those permanently subtidal under-surfaces of floating docks, ships' moorings, and channel buoys.

The smaller slugs (2 to 5 mm) are difficult to spot in tangles of algae, hydroids, bryozoans, and sponges, and even the larger species are often well camouflaged by closely resembling the shape and colour of their prey. However, sea slugs often advertise their presence by their white egg masses, which, like the gelatinous spawn of frogs, absorb water and swell up to a size several times that of the egg layer. So whenever you notice egg masses, collect that patch of alga or animal colony, put it in a shallow pan, and examine closely with the aid of a hand lens, reading glass, or jeweler's lens. Then let the tray stand for several hours on a shaded counter top. As the seawater warms and oxygen levels decrease, all kinds of creatures, including several species of sea slugs, will crawl out of the tangle and congregate at the surface where there is oxygen. Specimens may be kept live in marine aquaria or, more conveniently if you want to examine and photograph them over several days, in a clean jar half-filled with seawater and stored in a refrigerator.

If you are fortunate enough to live near the sea shore or have a summer cottage on the coast, you should experiment with this ingenious technique for growing your own sea slugs and other marine creatures. Stuff a small-mesh onion bag with scraps of fishermen's monofilament gill netting found about fishing villages or washed up on a beach. Hang this bag in the sea, and planktonic larvae of all sorts, including sponges, bryozoans, hydroids, crustaceans, starfish, molluscs, and so on, will drift through the bag mesh, settle on the fish net, and grow. Most will grow too large to escape back out through the mesh or will remain because of all the food available. It takes about two months for the action to pick up, but each time you haul in and examine your invertebrate condominium it will be a surprise as to who the tenants will be. Place pieces of the fish net in a deep tray of seawater, examine bushy growths, and look closely for crawling sea beauties. You could discover a real rarity. These mesh bags can be left out all winter, and by April will have lots of cold-water spawners at maximum sizes.

RECORD KEEPING

To fully appreciate the form and pigment patterns of sacoglossans and nudibranchs, examine them with a binocular microscope whenever possible. At this time you should make sketches and record colours of the live animals and note behaviour patterns during feeding, breeding, or spawning. Add this information to your record book or data sheet and also record when, where, and how you found them. The most difficult but most rewarding method of record keeping is to photograph these extravagant organisms live. See Appendix 1 on page 196 for a diagram and description of one photographic setup that works well. You will also need cool, filtered seawater (keep a stock in the refrigerator), a quiet room, and lots of patience. Save some of the algae or animal colonies upon which you found the slugs feeding. This should be preserved with the slugs for later examination or identification, and you may want to use some as macrophotography background. If you are into scuba diving and underwater macrophotography, then you can venture well beyond the intertidal and seek nudibranchs and photo opportunities in the undersea realm.

PRESERVING

For those seriously interested in establishing a reference collection of preserved opisthobranchs,

I recommend they first contact a science museum or university biology department and learn something of the proper types of jars, vials, paper, and ink required for long-term storage. The slugs should be preserved in 70% ethyl alcohol with a label of water-resistant paper and waterproof ink naming the species and where, when, and by whom it was collected. This should be done so that specimens are available for further anatomical studies and for species verification. Be aware that once opisthobranchs are preserved, their lovely form and colour are lost—hence the inestimable value of colour photographs or paintings. You should always offer to donate a duplicate set of specimens to a provincial or national museum where the curatorial staff and facilities can assure the proper, long-term storage of specimens in liquid. Too often, private collections become neglected, dry up, and are tossed out and thereby lost forever.

The quickest way to preserve fresh specimens is to drop them into 70% alcohol. They will, however, contract into an unidentifiable blob. A better method, and one that retains as near as natural form as possible, is the more humane technique of freezing the specimens in seawater in a shallow jar lid. They will simply slow down and then freeze in their natural extended position. Then pour 5 to 10% Formalin (or alcohol or vinegar, or even whiskey in a dire emergency) over the ice and return to the freezer. Remove from freezer in 10 to 15 minutes, allow ice to melt, pour off half the water, and replace it with 70% alcohol for half an hour before storing in pure 70% alcohol. Animals prepared in this manner are then convenient to examine and dissect, as often must be done for precise species identification.

IDENTIFYING

Most identification difficulties will occur within species, because there can be several distinct colour phases that look as if they should be another species. The initial point of comparison to rely upon is the basic body shape (morphology) of each major group, genus, or species. Sort out the colour variations later, and discover that in *Acanthodoris pilosa* (p. 75) colour varieties abound and are of no taxonomic significance and probably only reflect what that nudibranch is eating this week. In contrast, almost every colour pattern variation in the genus *Eubranchus* (pp. 127–139) actually is a distinct species with different teeth and different arrangement of internal organs, neither of which can be detected with a hand lens.

The usual and easiest way to identify something collected at the seashore is to look it up in a field guide book. Not so for nudibranchs and sacoglossans. As a consequence of there having been too few expert Canadian sluggers in the past, there is not much information to put in an Atlantic coast field guide. There are a few colour plates in American seashore guides, but often our more common species are not included. The Nova Scotia Museum and the Royal Ontario Museum have on file a set of colour prints and colour transparencies of many of our Atlantic Canada species. The ring-bound book *Keys to the Flora and Fauna of Minas Basin* is a useful reference for Canadian sea slugs and is particularly valuable for identification of the plant and animal species upon which they feed. The recent publication (1994) of a colour field guide to 108 species of nudibranchs of the British Isles will prove useful. The excellent photos include 24 of our local species, and many of the other illustrations hint at what may yet be discovered on this side of the Atlantic. Unfortunately, the guide omits journal references, taxonomic treatment, and species from the orders Thecosomata, Gymnosomata, and Sacoglossa.

For more information you will have to consult the sorts of books and journals listed in the section References for Particular Species. These books and journals are usually available at university libraries, museum libraries, or marine stations and oceanographic institutions. And don't be shy about knocking on the doors of such intimidating institutions, because they actually like to encourage young, potential marine scientists.

There are three additional lists at the end of this book: References—General; References—Sacoglossa (=Ascoglossa); and References—Field Guides, all of which will provide a wealth of answers and lead you on to other sources. As your most direct and thorough introduction to the real world of opisthobranch research, I recommend the special T. E. Thompson Memorial Issue of the *British Journal of Molluscan Studies,* Volume 57, Part 4, November 1991. The 23 articles spread over 242 pages may astound you with their diversity of subject matter and breadth of global geography.

Many of our local species are easily recognized with the naked eye or a hand lens. But to identify every sacoglossan and nudibranch or other opisthobranch that you may find, would require a large library of rare old texts, numerous journal reprints, about 10 years' experience, access to standard equipment of a modern biology laboratory, and a $60,000 scanning electron microscope. The latter piece of apparatus is essential for examination of the tiny teeth on the rasping tongue of these molluscs, a feature of utmost importance in their classification.

When in doubt as to an identification, consult your local science museum or institute for more information and for names and addresses of specialists who would be interested in examining your finds. Several sea slugs new to science have been discovered in Nova Scotia and in New England, and undoubtedly there will be more. Imagine, you might be so lucky as to have a scientist name a slug after you!

Beginner's Pictorial Key to Sea Slugs

There are 23 genera pictured here, but they can be sorted quite quickly by first choosing one of four habitat categories. Where did you find your specimen:

Group 1, in the open ocean,
Group 2, on green plants,
Group 3, on a rock, or
Group 4, on a bushy growth of colonial animals?

At our present stage of knowledge of these intriguing animals you can expect many specimens to be easily identified, others to be quite difficult, and others simply impossible—quite simply because you are the first person to ever find one of that kind. The only coastlines on our planet that could be considered well surveyed are those of England and California. So, why not become a marine biologist, specialize in opisthobranch biology, and contribute some immortal discovery to science and for Canada.

GROUP 1 *Seen swimming in the ocean, these species look like little butterflies and are found in company with jellyfish and comb jellies and other plankton. You only see these species over the side of a boat or beneath you when snorkeling or above you when scuba diving.*

GROUP 2 *You will discover these slugs feeding on green plant matter, usually filamentous green algae, either in tidal marshes or along rocky coasts. The one exception is* Elysia catula, *which spends its entire life on blades of eelgrass.*

Ercolania
6mm, p. 56

Alderia
10mm, p. 50

GROUP 3 *These chunky animals are found on the flat surfaces of rocks, wharf pilings, kelp blades, and such. They all have a posterior, middorsal circle of feathery gills, in the centre of which is the anus.*

Ancula
20mm, p. 69

Okenia
10mm, p. 72

GROUP 4 *Look for these beautiful bushy-backed animals on bushy animal colonies, such as hydroids, sea anemones, and ectoprocts, all of which grow on rocks, wharfs, floating docks, channel buoys, and ships' hulls.*

4a *The projections on the back are branched like a tree or knobby like a pineapple.*

4b *The projections on the back are simple, unbranched, and finger-like.*

Cuthona
5-15mm, p. 140

Coryphella
20-40mm, p. 113

Eubranchus
5-15mm, p. 127

Tenellia
5mm, p. 155

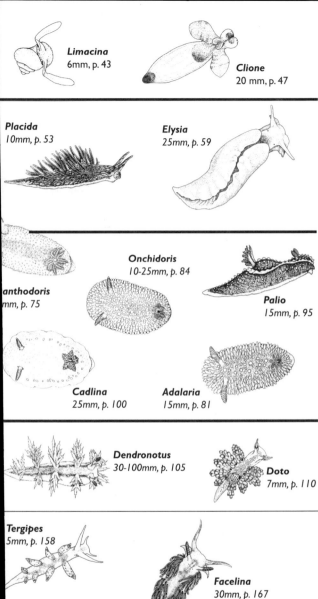

Limacina
6mm, p. 43

Clione
20 mm, p. 47

Placida
10mm, p. 53

Elysia
25mm, p. 59

Onchidoris
10-25mm, p. 84

anthodoris
mm, p. 75

Palio
15mm, p. 95

Cadlina
25mm, p. 100

Adalaria
15mm, p. 81

Dendronotus
30-100mm, p. 105

Doto
7mm, p. 110

Tergipes
5mm, p. 158

Facelina
30mm, p. 167

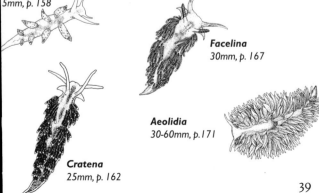

Aeolidia
30-60mm, p.171

Cratena
25mm, p. 162

Species Accounts: Descriptions and Comments

On the following pages you will find separate
text descriptions of 42 species (although in total
47 species are discussed). Each includes a black and
white illustration, a classification and scientific name,
a brief anatomical description, notes on natural history and known distribution, and a comments section.

The natural history information is supplemented
by Figure 3 (p.42), which compares the seasonal
occurrence of species based on a four-year study
in Connecticut with what little is known from our
Atlantic Canada records. There are many blank
months, chiefly because few persons are dedicated,
year-round sluggers.

The distribution paragraph usually includes two categories, worldwide distribution and local reports, both of
which need augmenting. In fact, maps depicting the distributions of many marine organisms should not be
considered definitive, for it is the distribution of biologists that they depict. Possibly the highest correlation
coefficients in science are those between species distributions and the distributions of biologists' summer
cottages.

In the comments you will be introduced, via that particular species, to a particular aspect of the biological
sciences such as a principle, a theory, a problem, a con-
troversy, a mystery, a challenge, or a technique. The
broad spectrum of truly relevant topics may seem im-
pressive for such an "obscure" group of molluscs,
but this diversity is typical of subject matter that the

research "specialist" will utilize. The lesson thus learned is perhaps unexpected: becoming a specialist actually expands one's awareness and appreciation of many other subjects.

Whenever you see a name inserted in the text accompanied by a year date (often in brackets), you will know who was responsible for discovering the facts under discussion and in what year they published that information. If you want to read that particular scientific article or book, it will be found under the author's name in one or more of the four lists of References.

FIG.3 Seasonal Occurrence of West Atlantic Sea Slugs

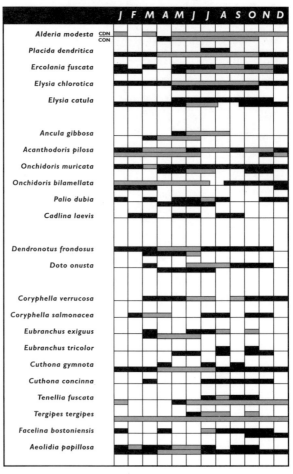

A chart of seasonal occurrence of those species for which there is some information. Canadian data (CAN) is graphed above the horizontal line, and comparative Connecticut, U.S.A., data (CON) from Clark, 1975, is depicted on the lower side of the same line. The months in which adults and spawn were found are grey bars. Solid bars indicate additional months in which juveniles and/or adults were collected. For most of these species, there are obvious information gaps.

Limacina retroversa

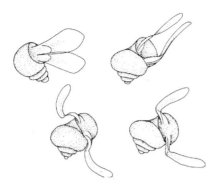

Order: **Thecosomata**
Family: Limacinidae
Genus: *Limacina (=spiratella)*
Species: *retroversa*
Authority: (Fleming, 1823)
Species: *helicina*
Authority: (Phipps, 1774)

DESCRIPTION

To 11 mm, but usually 2 to 6 mm. In life they appear to be tiny black butterflies fluttering beneath the water surface, hence their common name of sea butterfly. Spiral shell is extremely thin and fragile. Foot is small but surmounted by one pair of large, thin but muscular, epipodial wings. Shell of *retroversa* has a spire, whereas that of *helicina* is nearly flat.

NATURAL HISTORY

These snails are always at sea, forever swimming, never crawling. As their floating ribbons of eggs are part of the plankton, they are termed holo-plank-tonic gastropods. This sea slug family is very unusual, for it does not rely upon that basic rasping tongue of gastropods for feeding. Most opisthobranchs either rasp away at other animals or pierce the cell walls of plants, but *Limacina* uses cilia and mucus (as do clams) to capture microscopic phytoplankton. It is a prime herbivore feeding at the very base of the oceanic food pyramid and consequently can generate phenomenal population densities. In fact, oceanographers consider *L. retroversa* to be the most abundant pelagic gastropod in the world. Yet few seashore naturalists are aware of these sea butterflies, chiefly because they usually occur offshore and underwater. However, unlike much zooplankton, which daily migrates to deeper water in daylight, the thecosomes are active near the surface even at midday and can be dip-netted from off the side of a small boat.

You are more likely to discover a swarm along an exposed shore, or sometimes in large bays, occasionally from a wharf, and more rarely stranded in a tide pool of the Bay of Fundy coast. If you do much scuba diving or even snorkeling in our cold coastal waters, look for pelagic snails in association with swarms of the more conspicuous jellyfish and comb jellies.

DISTRIBUTION

Limacina retroversa occurs in the temperate North Atlantic, north to southern Greenland, and in the subantarctic oceans, but not in the North Pacific. *Limacina helicina* is a cold-water species common in the North Atlantic, North Pacific, Arctic, and Antarctic oceans.

COMMENTS

These wing-footed opisthobranchs are a select group of relatively few species but are astronomical in their abundance over most of the world's oceans. Analysis of the stomach contents of salmon, seabirds, baleen whales, and basking sharks indicates that thecosomes can be a major prey item. The nearly extinct northern right whale and Arctic bowhead whale depended heavily upon sea butterflies. The recently discovered population of northern right whales at the mouth of the Bay of Fundy, which had somehow avoided detection and extermination by whalers, has probably been dependent upon swarms of little *Limacina retroversa* for its very survival.

The mental image that most of us have of the open ocean is of a clear blue-green liquid, which makes it difficult to visualize concentrations of plankton across miles of ocean that turn the water into a veritable seafood chowder. *Limacina* often occurs in densities of 12,000/m³ in these chowders, and it is only one of dozens of nutritious items in that same cubic metre. Naval divers have told me of visual problems during inspection of ships' hulls underwater when swarms of pteropods, jellyfish, comb jellies, copepods, and shrimps were so dense that they could not see their hand when their arm was extended. Imagine what happens to soft plankton creatures when a baleen whale scoops up a ton of this chowder, presses it against the baleen screens, scrapes off the residue animal concentrate with its tongue, and funnels all into its churning stomach. The jellyfish are a write-off. About the only organisms that are still recognizable are the hard-shelled crustaceans. This is why in most natural history books and field guides about all that is mentioned as food of whales are crustaceans such as copepods, shrimp, or krill. Obviously, any stomach contents paste that contains crustaceans is also made up of those many fragile organisms, now essentially unidentifiable. However, should the opportunity ever arise to examine a baleen whale's stomach, you should now recognize the little black fragments as the body and wings of a sea butterfly.

Clione limacina

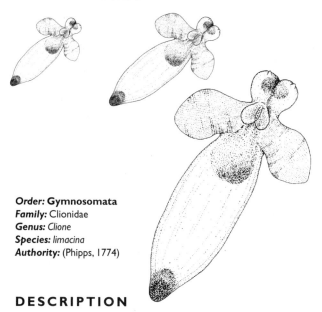

Order: **Gymnosomata**
Family: Clionidae
Genus: *Clione*
Species: *limacina*
Authority: (Phipps, 1774)

DESCRIPTION

To 22 mm. A shell-less, translucent and transparent, elongate squid-shaped sea slug, with one pair of oval wings at the narrow neck constriction between head and body. This bizarre creature would be invisible in the water were it not for the bright red-orange colour of structures inside the head, and the orange liver and pigment cap at the tip of the body cone. Within the large head are stored six retracted tentacles and two bundles of feeding hooks.

NATURAL HISTORY

Wherever you find swarms of the thecosome sea butterfly *Limacina*, you will also find *Clione limacina*, for it feeds on nothing else and thereby gained its species designation of "limacina." This streamlined menace can cruise slowly or swim quickly, steering with its "tail," and easily outmanoeuvres the shelled

Limacina. Upon contact with its prey, the six tentacles are protruded, and as these curve around the *Limacina* snail shell, they grip it through a combination of sticky adhesive and minute suction cups. *Clione* then everts the two bundles of hooks and drives these into the soft body of *Limacina*, which then is pulled from its shell and swallowed whole. (There is a closely related genus, *Crucibranchaea*, that possesses two long tentacles equipped with large, stalked suction cups [Figure 1]. Those arms are astounding miniature replicas of the arms of an octopus—certainly not what you would expect from a slug!)

Because there is a limitless supply of *Limacina* in the world's seas, the carnivorous *Clione* and relatives can afford to superspecialize their anatomy and become totally dependent upon only one prey item. In a way *Clione limacina* has it made, but how much time must it spend glancing over its shoulder on the lookout for a competing specialist—the baleen whale?

DISTRIBUTION

This single species probably ranges worldwide, for what were once considered separate species, such as Atlantic and Pacific ocean populations, are now included within *Clione limacina*.

COMMENTS

The red-orange *Clione* are conspicuous in a swarm of the smaller, black *Limacina*, but always there are very few *Clione*. The ratios of the herbivorous *Limacina* to the carnivorous *Clione* (survey figures range from 12:1 to over 600:1) are superb examples of what the theoretical models predict, for when food is consumed, less than 10 per cent is actually converted to new animal tissue. This means that starting with a finite number of plants per hectare, only 10 per cent can become real solid herbivore tissue, and only 10 per cent of that 10 per cent can become new carnivore tissue, and so on, carnivore by carnivore level. Thus at each feeding step (termed trophic levels) the amount of solar energy captured by the plants is very rapidly reduced and can support but fewer and fewer carnivores. On land the levels might be plants, deer, wolves, period: there is nothing that lives on a diet of wolves. Our Canadian Atlantic and Arctic waters, in contrast, are really remarkable, for their phytoplankton supports an unbelievable series of small to large carnivores: plants to crustaceans, to small carnivorous fish and seabirds, to larger fish and seabirds, to seals and porpoises, and finally to polar bears and killer whales. And consider as well the giant grazers such as the basking shark and the baleen whales, which grab tons of the chowder while it is still fresh in the pot.

Can you imagine the catastrophic consequences of the destruction of ocean plankton—everything from sea slugs to whales would starve to death. Such a cataclysmic extinction did occur in the Permian Period, over 200 million years ago, and nearly 95 per cent of all marine invertebrate species were terminated. Were the only species that did survive specialists in feeding upon dead bodies?

Alderia modesta

Order: Sacoglossa
Family: Stiligeridae
Genus: *Alderia*
Species: *modesta*
Authority: (Lovén, 1844)

DESCRIPTION

To 18 mm, but usually 5 to 8 mm. A drab, mottled, little brown slug, occasionally varying to pale cream, in which case the branching green gut tract is evident.

There is a rhythmical contraction of the cerata on one side of the body alternating with those on the other. It is this alternating pulsing that circulates blood through the animal's body, for during development its heart atrophies and is totally absent in the adult. Another, more obvious yet invisible, diagnostic characteristic is a potent, sickly-sweet perfume exuded by this sacoglossan. The origin, chemistry, and function of this highly volatile compound are unknown.

NATURAL HISTORY

This heartless slug is strictly a resident of tidal and estuarine marshes where it feeds upon the alga *Vaucheria*. In Minas Basin the alga forms green, velvet-like mats on the marsh in summer but in winter survives in the deeper marsh pools as tangles of long filaments. *Alderia* occurs in both habitats and in summer lays club-shaped, gelatinous egg masses on *Vaucheria* mats exposed to the air between tides. In autumn and early spring the egg masses are laid on submerged algae in the pools. This truly amphibious sea slug may spend weeks in the upper marshgrass zone without experiencing tidal submergence. In summer *Alderia* probably spends more time out of water than under. Perhaps its "perfume" is actually part of a chemical defence armoury, for it shares the marshgrass habitat with predaceous spiders, beetles, and bugs.

Alderia seems always to be laying eggs, with records from nearly every month of the year, including December and January. This species wastes no time in ritual courtship, as do many molluscs, but transfers sperm to other individuals in seconds through hypodermic insemination. It simply jabs its hypodermic-needle penis into another *Alderia* absolutely anywhere, be it the head, cerata, foot, or tail, and then pumps in a mass of sperm. This is a bizarre method of copulation, but even more perplexing is how the sperm ever find their way through a maze of living tissue to the ovary.

DISTRIBUTION

Alderia modesta occurs in coastal marshes of
Europe, in eastern North America from Newfoundland to New York State, and on the west coast
from British Columbia to California. Ask yourself,
"How does an animal that lives only in tidal marshes
get from one marsh to another, and halfway around the
world?" You might also ask another unanswered question: "Why after all this time, and over that vast distance,
is it still only the one species?" *Alderia modesta* may be
such an ancient species that it was a marsh specialist even
prior to the "recent" continental drifting that formed the
Atlantic Ocean, about 180 million years ago.

COMMENTS

This unique, sweet-smelling, heartless, amphibious
sea slug is really quite common but has a century-
old history of being overlooked by marine
biologists. This is because most marine biologists
simply rush across tidal marshes to get to the sea,
and the only ones that actually stop and study
marshes are botanists.

Alderia modesta was first noticed in Norway and
England in 1844, then found in marshes at Cam-
bridge, Massachusetts, in 1848, then on Grand
Manan Island, New Brunswick, in 1853. It was not
reported again in North America until discovered
in California in 1955 and then "rediscovered" on
our east coast (Nova Scotia, this time) in 1965.
Since then, a few marine zoologists with an insatiable curiosity about tidal marshes have shown that
coastal marshes of New Brunswick, Prince Edward
Island, Nova Scotia, and Newfoundland are teeming with this "very rare species." Undoubtedly it
has always been there.

Placida dendritica

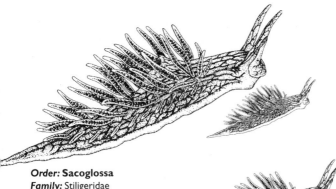

Order: Sacoglossa
Family: Stiligeridae
Genus: *Placida* (=*Hermaea*)
Species: *dendritica*
Authority: (Alder & Hancock, 1843)

DESCRIPTION

To 20 mm, but usually 5 to 8 mm. Translucent, ivory-coloured body with many projecting cerata and a green gut tract that ramifies throughout the body, branching even into the rhinophore tentacles. Single pair of head tentacles (rhinophores) that are in-rolled, forming a trough. A middorsal tubular anus in front of the bulbous heart region. Two conditions that can confuse the beginner slug watcher occur when the typical long tail has been broken off short and when the entire animal appears yellowish from not feeding upon green algae.

NATURAL HISTORY

This sacoglossan feeds on green algae of the genera *Codium*, *Bryopsis*, and *Derbesia* but does not maintain functional chloroplasts in its tissues. When this species of slug was discovered in Nova Scotia in the

1970s, *Codium* was absent from Atlantic Canada, and as *Bryopsis* is rare, it was only from *Derbesia* that *P. dendritica* was collected. The alga *Derbesia* forms small tufts of green filaments, which attach to rocks, mussel shells, tunicate cases, and the surface of other alga, so more luck than skill was involved in finding this combination of slug and alga. However, since the early 1990s there has been a dramatic change. Big, bushy green *Codium* has invaded Nova Scotia, and it is rapidly spreading up that Atlantic coastline and washing ashore conspicuously on our beaches. Does this new larder of favourite succulent alga portend our "extremely rare" *P. dendritica* will soon become "extremely common?"

In Connecticut, where *P. dendritica* feeds upon *Codium fragile*, the adults appear suddenly in March, and egg laying peaks in June but can extend into October. There are far fewer animals by then, and by mid-December the entire population has vanished. The sudden appearance of large adults "out of nowhere" has been observed in several other slug species and is an unsolved mystery. Where have the juveniles been feeding and growing, and how do they travel to arrive so suddenly each year? It can be as long as two months between the time the slugs were last found and the start of another adult invasion.

DISTRIBUTION

Mediterranean Sea, Atlantic and Pacific oceans (in fact, from Newfoundland to New Zealand), from tropical to boreal waters. Probably the most widely distributed species of sea slug. Rare in our area, so far: Logy Bay, Newfoundland; Annapolis Basin, Chester Basin, and Isaacs Harbour, Nova Scotia.

COMMENTS

This species is of considerable interest to scholars of natural selection and evolutionary processes, for worldwide *P. dendritica*'s anatomy has remained uniform. Most sea slugs (and most animals, for that matter) have evolved different species in different parts of the world. The only difference detected in this sacoglossan is in the fine cutting edge of its teeth. Atlantic Ocean specimens have conical denticles, whereas Pacific Ocean samples exhibit smaller truncate denticles. This probably is the consequence of a minor mutation that occurred in a population of *P. dendritica* that was the first to populate the newly forming Atlantic Ocean, some 180 million years ago. Only one tiny mutation over tens of millions of years is proof that it can happen and also proof that evolutionary clocks based on mutation rates are not universally applicable. Neither does it mean that this species of sacoglossan has lost all ability to adapt, for it has the unusual capability of adjusting the size of its teeth and the rate at which they are produced in response to the toughness of the algae it eats.

Ercolania fuscata

Order: Sacoglossa
Family: Stiligeridae
Genus: Ercolania (=Stiliger)
Species: fuscata
Authority: Gould, 1870

DESCRIPTION

To 8 mm, but usually 4 to 6 mm. A velvet-black to
grey-green, incessantly active little slug, with cerata
limited to posterior two-thirds of the body. Tips of
cerata, sole of foot, and an elongate area around
each black eye are pale cream colour. The branching, green gut tract is usually well masked by the fine
cross-banding of black pigment at the skin's surface.

NATURAL HISTORY

This species feeds on the filamentous algae
Cladophora and *Chaetomorpha* by piercing algal
cells and sucking out the contents. These empty
cells then constitute weak points, and the filament
may break under stress of wave action. When many
E. fuscatua congregate and feed at the base of an
algal tuft, the entire algal colony may break loose.
By late summer, there are floating mats of these

green algae drifting back and forth within bays and along the coast. So not only are these tiny sea slugs major grazers of algae, they also cut quantities of algae adrift, thereby adding considerably to the energy pool of flotsam and detritus.

In Connecticut, this sea slug could not be found from December to June, yet every June and July adults appeared and laid. Those eggs quickly hatched, and in three to four weeks the new slugs were 7 mm long and were in turn laying eggs.

In contrast, in Atlantic Canada, this species has been collected in Minas Basin every month of the year except February and April. The habitat is permanent pools of the tidal marsh, where there is usually an abundance of various filamentous algae. However, these little black slugs are most conspicuous as they crawl about on the open silty bottoms of these tidal pools. If they are feeding from the mud, their algal prey must be very young filaments of *Cladophora* and *Chaetomorpha* or something else unsuspected such as diatoms or desmids.

DISTRIBUTION

Nova Scotia to Virginia, Mexico, and southeast Australia. This apparently patchy distribution has two possible explanations. First there have not been enough slug watchers worldwide to search every coastline and fill in the gaps. Second, examination of old museum specimens may reveal misidentified *E. fuscata* from intermediate geographic areas.

Reported in Nova Scotia from tidal marshes of Minas Basin, Kings County, the coast of Lunenburg County, Halifax County, and Guysborough County and from Malpeque Bay, Prince Edward Island.

COMMENTS

This species of algal sapsucker is a recent addition to the tidal marsh fauna of Minas Basin. One specimen turned up in algal samples in 1970, then several specimens in 1972, and by late 1973 it could be collected by the hundreds and has remained relatively abundant ever since. Where did it come from? Why has it stayed in Minas Basin? What is its impact as a herbivore? We simply do not know.

There is an interesting lesson to be learned from this species of sacoglossan: faunal composition can change locally over the short term without human alteration of the environment. (See comments under *Elysia chlorotica* for a similar phenomenon noted at the Lawrencetown Beach area, Halifax County.) Marine ecosystems certainly are persistent, but their working components, namely the various species of plants and animals, normally exhibit both subtle and dramatic variations in their comings and goings and stayings. Once you realize this you can appreciate how difficult, if not impossible, it is for biologists to predict with any real confidence what will change if a harbour, a causeway, or a tidal power generator is built.

Elysia chlorotica

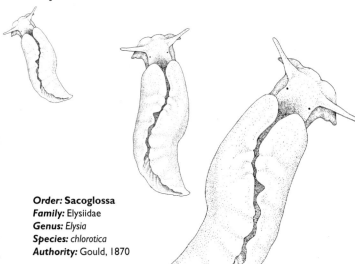

Order: **Sacoglossa**
Family: Elysiidae
Genus: *Elysia*
Species: *chlorotica*
Authority: Gould, 1870

DESCRIPTION

To 45 mm, but more often in the 5 to 25 mm range.
Normally an allover, emerald green, but the green
can be greyish or reddish. Scattered over the body
are conspicuous white blotches, and between these
are many inconspicuous tiny red dots. On slugs devoid of green chlorophyll (a rare condition), the
numerous red dots impart a rusty hue to the otherwise
cream-coloured animal.

The body is actually flat and heart shaped, but the
two lateral body extensions are usually folded over
the body, forming a tube. On the inner walls of this
tube is a branching pattern formed by large blood
vessels that also serve as gills.

NATURAL HISTORY

This sacoglossan has been referred to poetically as a "leaf that crawls," not only because of the leaf-like shape and venation, but also because of its remarkable photosynthetic capabilities. *Elysia chlorotica* slices into and then sucks the sap from cells of the intertidal alga *Vaucheria*. Then, by mysterious physiological processes, the slug incorporates the consumed but somehow undigested chloroplasts into its gut tract cells, where they happily continue to produce carbohydrates in the presence of sunlight. These stolen chloroplasts ("kleptoplastids") can function within the sacoglossan tissues for months, and their by-products become slug mucus. This is of significant benefit to the slug, because mucus production is one of the most energy-consuming of physiological activities.

Besides eating algae and farming their chloroplasts, this sea slug may also absorb dissolved free amino acids from the seawater in contact with its skin and from these already prefabricated pieces quickly construct its own proteins. This third nutritional mode as been detected in *Elysia subornata* from Florida, but other species in this genus have yet to be investigated.

Because *E. chlorotica* is large, bright green, and readily accessible in tidal marshes, pools, and creeks, it should be easy to study. Well, it isn't. The true life history of this sacoglossan remains a mystery. Available literature suggests that it may be an annual species attaining its maximum size in autumn, at which time it spawns and dies. However, long-term observations (1965–92) in Minas Basin, Nova Scotia, indicate otherwise, for egg strings were found from May through October and large adults (35 to 45 mm) from May through January.

In winter, slugs were located by cutting through the ice cover of marsh pools. On one occasion, *Elysia* were observed in pockets on the underside of ice blocks, presumably there for the benefit of their sun-loving chloroplasts.

In some field samples all specimens are of similar size, at other times many size classes are represented, and this can vary from place to place and year to year. *Elysia* can be common or even abundant in an area for years and then suddenly disappear. That is comprehensible, but the phenomenon of hordes of 35- to 45-mm long *E. chlorotica* suddenly appearing, seemingly overnight, in creeks and marsh pools is incomprehensible. No one has discovered just where they accomplish such maximal growth, nor by what magical means they are zapped onto the marshes. This usually happens in late October or early November in Nova Scotia and Massachusetts.

In 1985 we learned that even where and when these invasions may occur can be unpredictable. The Conrad Beach marsh pool area near Lawrencetown, Halifax County, had been sampled regularly since 1966 without discovery of a single *Elysia*. Field biologists were, therefore, astounded in June 1985 at the spectacle of thousands of large *E. chlorotica* all through the marsh. These concentrations continued throughout the summer, at least into late August when sampling ceased. One site was revisited in 1986, '87, and '88, but the *Elysia* had abandoned those particular marshes. However, in June 1990, *Elysia chlorotica* were suddenly and abundantly present at nearby Chezzetcook Inlet.

In dramatic contrast, in June of 1983 and '84 in western Minas Basin marshes, all the *E. chlorotica* were small, and most lacked the green chlorophyll

(Gibson, Toews, and Bleakney, 1986).

Between 1982 and 1983, one population in Minas Basin had inexplicably doubled its average complement of radular teeth from 40 to 80 (Raymond and Bleakney, 1987).

In Massachusetts, two genetically different populations of *E. chlorotica* were discovered in 1980. From the eggs of one hatched planktonic larvae, from eggs of the other emerged tiny slugs (West, Harrington, and Pierce, 1984).

The more we learn about this species, the less we understand.

DISTRIBUTION

Endemic to east coast of North America from Nova Scotia to North Carolina. Although first described in 1870, this species was subsequently overlooked and not even included in the 1954 edition of Abbott's *American Seashells*. The first captures in Canada were in 1965 in Nova Scotia and now include the counties of Cape Breton, Richmond, Pictou, Halifax, and Kings. In 1969 *E. chlorotica* was found at Malpeque Bay, Prince Edward Island, and will undoubtedly turn up in New Brunswick.

COMMENTS

For hundreds of years biologists in Europe knew that many species of *Elysia* ate algae and consequently were green because their gut tract was visible through their translucent skin. It was not until the late 1960s that the unthinkable was discovered—the alga continues to function after it is eaten. Thus was the ultimate science-fiction monster revealed in our very midst—an animal with green photosynthetic skin. Only now, some 30 years later, is this remarkable discovery becoming incorporated into academic texts and natural history accounts.

More recently, in the mid-1980s, biochemists at the National Research Council laboratories in Halifax discovered that *Elysia chlorotica* protects its precious chloroplasts from harmful ultraviolet wavelengths by generating two very effective UV-absorbing screens (but why two?). One of these compounds was previously identified in a Hawaiian sacoglossan, but the other is a unique polyproprionate compound henceforth to be referred to officially as "elysione."

The same Halifax biochemists discovered potent antibiotic activity in the mucus of *Elysia chlorotica*. The erythromycin-like compound, something typically found in moulds not in molluscs, is the same proprionate UV-absorbing compound, elysione. It performs double duty. The mucoid coat of many aquatic animals serves to keep infectious bacteria and fungi from reaching their skin tissues. As aquarium enthusiasts know, if fish accidentally break this coat, an infection soon develops. Scientists now realize that to be effective these slimy coats must contain antibacterial, antifungal, antiviral, antiultraviolet, and other such agents. It is the actual chemical configuration of these compounds that is often so startling and unexpected, and that may even break new chemical or medical ground.

Elysia chlorotica also has a potent antipredator deterrent. Drop this creature into a fish tank, and immediately it is gobbled up and just as quickly spat out. The sacoglossan then sinks serenely to the tank bottom and thereafter crawls about the aquarium with impunity, never to be molested again by those particular fish. Neither the compound nor its provenance have been investigated. It may well be derived from the *Vaucheria* alga that *E. chlorotica* eats, because even brainless algae know that it pays to be undelicious, and they have evolved their own repulsive compounds. The tropical alga *Halimedae* produces a noxious diterpenoid that repels herbivorous fish. However, *Elysia halimedae* eats that alga with gusto and then very effectively concentrates the fish toxin in its mucous glands and even in its strings of eggs.

When you think of it, there *is* a lot of seaweed out there that nothing seems to eat. Makes you wonder whether a diet of dulse could keep mosquitos at bay.

Elysia catula

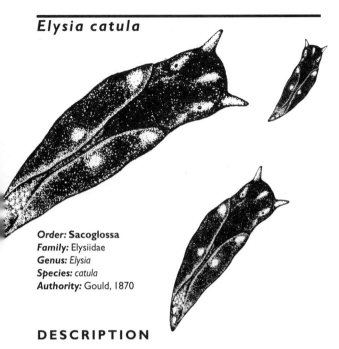

Order: Sacoglossa
Family: Elysiidae
Genus: *Elysia*
Species: *catula*
Authority: Gould, 1870

DESCRIPTION

To 6 mm, stocky and black and easily mistaken
for a shelled snail. Close examination reveals
the general dark green hue of the body and the pale
olive-green foot over which are scattered flecks of
white pigment. Greenish white areas are located as
follows: (1) at the tips of the tentacles, (2) one between the tentacles, (3) a diagonal pair posterior to
the tentacles, (4) a small pair at the anterior border of
the parapodial folds, (5) another pair midway along
the parapodia, and (6) an area at the tip of the tail.

In the head region, the combination of two slanted
eye patches and the ear-like tentacles is so evocative
of a black-faced Halloween cat that Mr. Gould
could not resist naming this diminutive sacoglossan
cat-ula, "little cat."

NATURAL HISTORY

Elysia catula is a unique sacoglossan specialist, for it feeds on the cell sap of the flowering plant *Zostera marina*, commonly referred to as eelgrass. Not a grass at all, *Zostera* is itself unusual for being a marine seed plant, a true flowering member of phylum Spermatophyta and closely related to the *Potamogeton* pond weeds. The only sacoglossan capable of puncturing the tough cuticle and cell walls of eelgrass is *E. catula,* and for this purpose its teeth are exceptionally sturdy.

In Connecticut this slug is an annual species, where spawning occurs in June and July, and the adults then die of "old age." The egg strings, containing as many as 1,000 eggs, are deposited as spirals on the narrow leaves of *Zostera*. Juveniles can be found in August and September, and they grow rapidly through October and November. In winter, *E. catula* retreats into crevices between the basal leaves of the *Zostera* stalks. In spring and early summer, these little black slugs are conspicuously crawling about on the green eelgrass blades, but so are other black, similar-sized, shelled snails, so one must look very closely.

Whether the life history of *E. catula* in Atlantic Canada differs in any way from populations in Connecticut is not yet known. Populations in the Chester, Nova Scotia, area are active in May and June, absent in July, reappear in late August, and are then common through November. Winter collecting has not been attempted.

DISTRIBUTION

Although *Zostera* occurs along both east and
west coasts of the North Atlantic and North
Pacific oceans, as well as in the Mediterranean Sea,
E. catula is limited to our western Atlantic shores
from Nova Scotia to South Carolina. There is another sacoglossan species that feeds upon sea
grasses in Florida and the Caribbean, *Elysia serca*.
This southern animal is a pale edition of *E. catula,*
and some experts believe it is only a colour variety
or at best a subspecies of *E. catula.*

In Atlantic Canada, this species is undoubtedly
underrepresented in collections, because so much
coastal marine fieldwork takes place in the summer
period betweeen late June and late August, just when
the adult *E. catula* are experiencing their annual die-
off, and before the juveniles are large enough to be
noticed. Records at the Nova Scotia Museum and the
National Museum of Canada are all from the Atlantic
coast of Nova Scotia, from Richmond County to
Lunenburg County.

COMMENTS

You would have been hard pressed to find *E. catula*
in 1931 or '32 and even in the decade following.
A mysterious blight struck *Zostera* beds on both
sides of the Atlantic (but not in the Pacific nor in
the Mediterranean), and in two seasons this marine
plant was almost completely destroyed. A natural
ecological catastrophe of this magnitude has seldom
been observed. Several populations of animals, such as
the Brant goose, were dependent upon those extensive
coastal beds of *Zostera* and were devastated. The com-
mercially valuable bay scallop was another vulnerable

specialist, for it attaches to eelgrass blades, thus suspending itself above the otherwise suffocating estuarine silts.

Zostera began to reappear in 1945–50 and from 1951–53 experienced its greatest recovery, but even through the 1970s there were some areas still devoid of *Zostera* beds. It would be interesting to know whether the *Zostera marina* and *Elysia catula* reappear together. Because Atlantic Canada is probably still in the recovery phase, these peripheral populations of *Zostera* could be sampled and monitored and that interesting question answered.

Years ago, *Elysia catula* was actually fingered as the villain in the *Zostera* blight catastrophe. The prosecution set out to prove that because *E. catula* punctured holes in *Zostera* leaves, it must be the agent spreading the disease. The defence argued that guilt by association is inadmissible evidence and then cleverly tabled documents showing that the disease occurred simultaneously from Spain to Norway in 1931–32, and that *E. catula* does not occur in Europe, nor does any other *Zostera*- leaf-piercing sacoglossan. Case dismissed.

Ancula gibbosa

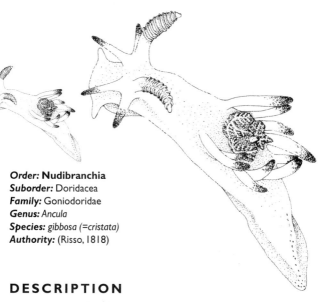

Order: **Nudibranchia**
Suborder: Doridacea
Family: Goniodoridae
Genus: *Ancula*
Species: *gibbosa (=cristata)*
Authority: (Risso, 1818)

DESCRIPTION

To 33 mm. Body white to translucent white, the only colour accent being the yellow or orange tips on all of the long, slender tubercles. There can be orange flecks on the gills and rhinophores, and a streak of orange flecks middorsally on the tail. The three tripinnate gills are flanked on each side with five to seven tall tubercles, and at the base of each rhinophore are two forward-projecting tubercles.

NATURAL HISTORY

This strikingly beautiful species is uncommon but when found by turning over rocks is usually abundant. It occurs from the intertidal to depths of over 100 metres. In Europe spawning is reported from February to November, but in Connecticut only from April through June. In Nova Scotia specimens were collected from May to late August and egg masses found in June, July, and August.

In Nova Scotia, this nudibranch was first found on the white sponge *Leucosolenia,* which seemed a reasonable colour camouflage, but then it was found on red algae, and then on hydroids. In Connecticut its prey is the tiny, colonial bryozoan *Bougainvillia* (phylum Ectoprocta), and in England, the flat, fleshy tunicate colonies of *Botryllus* and *Botrylloides* are preferred, while a report from the North Sea area claims *A. gibbosa* is herbivorous.

DISTRIBUTION

In Europe, from the Mediterranean Sea to Arctic Russia, east to Greenland, and south to Connecticut. In Atlantic Canada only from Kings, Digby, Lunenburg, and Halifax counties.

On our west coast, the species *Ancula pacifica* may some day turn out to be the European *A. gibbosa,* a global zoogeographic relationship having already been revealed for several other Northeast Pacific nudibranchs.

COMMENTS

As *Ancula gibbosa* is a summer species, here is a great project for an amateur marine naturalist who is fortunate enough to find a colony of this nudibranch. What does this slug really eat? It is impossible to believe that it can cut up and digest algae, bryozoans, tunicates, sponges, and hydroids. Just because you find a nudibranch sitting on something edible, you have no right to assume that that slug would give its right rhinophore for a lifetime supply of the stuff. It may simply be passing by or, more precisely, across. A better but not foolproof indication that such may be a preferred food is if the slug has deposited an egg mass on that item. But the only way to know for sure is to observe carefully and determine whether pieces are actually rasped out of the prey and consumed. Perhaps *A. gibbosa* does consume a diverse spectrum of foods, but such a diet would be unprecedented, and, if true, we will have to add another chapter to our ever-expanding collection of sea slug superlatives.

Okenia ascidicola

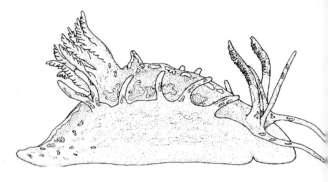

Order: Nudibranchia
Suborder: Doridacea
Family: Goniodorididae
Genus: Okenia
Species: ascidicola
Authority: M. P. Morse, 1972

DESCRIPTION

To 12 mm. Hump-backed body is a reddish brown,
paler at the sides, with rows of dark and light yellow
blotches. Yellow speckles decorate the tentacles.
At the sides, the high mantle edge has six long ten-
tacular appendages, and four others projecting
forward. The long rhinophores have about 25 shelf-
like lamellae on their posterior surface.

NATURAL HISTORY

This new species was discovered near Boston in
1968 but was not provided with a name until 1972.
How is it that after more than 100 years of intensive
biological investigation in the Boston and Cape Cod
area, Professor Patricia Morse could discover a new
species of nudibranch? It had been overlooked
because its special prey is a species of sea squirt

(a sessile tunicate of the Ascidiacea group) within the tunic of which it remains hidden as it feeds. This species' name means "to inhabit ascidians."

Professor Morse kept the two original animals in an aquarium, they fed, they exchanged sperm, they laid eggs, and the eggs hatched into veliger larvae. Thus, in one fortuitous fell swoop, she obtained data from all the life history stages of her new species.

In captivity the two sea slugs fed only upon the ascidian *Molgula manhattensis*, itself an inconspicuous sessile sac of an animal, its surface usually encrusted with debris. Peculiarly, this tunicate seems highly tolerant of both polluted and brackish waters. This *Okenia* fed by rasping a circular hole in the tough tunic sheath and then squeezed inside to feed on the softer body parts, leaving only its circle of gills projecting from the hole.

DISTRIBUTION

The first two and all subsequent specimens have been from the East Point, Nahant area of Massachusetts. Colonies of *Molgula manhattensis* and other suitably large species of tunicates should be examined carefully for this and other possibly undiscovered species of nudibranch predators. As *Okenia ascidicola* occurs near Boston, then it should also frequent other areas of the Gulf of Maine and Bay of Fundy.

COMMENTS

Although the tiny, tadpole-like larva of ascidian tunicates share basic features in common with chordates (including ourselves), the adult is a peculiar sessile sac, attached directly or by a stalk. The ascidian skin secretes a thick cellulose (yes, as in plants) tunic that encloses everything, the gill chamber, gut tract, gonads, and heart. Apparently, a few dorid nudibranchs occasionally eat species of small colonial tunicates that form crusts on rocks and wharf pilings, but the larger solitary tunicates are not listed as nudibranch prey. Their tough cellulose tunic would not be a deterrent against predators equipped with a molluscan radular rasp. So why are tunicates rarely on menus? Recent investigations at the National Research Council Laboratory, Halifax, demonstrated that solitary ascidian tunicates, as one might expect of a sessile bite-sized animal, are loaded with chemical deterrents. Perhaps *Okenia ascidicola* is a specialist that has managed to circumvent these toxins. It may well have the added ability to consume and sequester these deterrents within its own tissues for its own defence.

On the other hand, because the slug feeds ensconced within the ascidian tunic, it is already enshrouded by a sophisticated, toxic, cellulose armour of proven evolutionary effectiveness, so why waste valuable energy and resources on overkill?

Acanthodoris pilosa

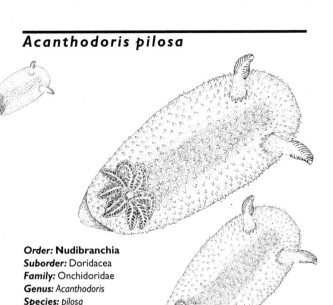

Order: **Nudibranchia**
Suborder: Doridacea
Family: Onchidoridae
Genus: Acanthodoris
Species: pilosa
Authority: (Müller, 1789)

DESCRIPTION

To 55 mm, but usually 15 to 25 mm. The mantle surface has an abundance of soft, conical papillae, the
tips of which are usually a pale to lemon yellow.
Rhinophores are bent back, and their basal sheath
has a tuberculate rim. A circle of up to nine large,
tripinnate gills. Anatomically this species is easy to
recognize, but chromatically it is a riot: the body
may be an all-over white or yellow or orange or grey
or brown or mauve or maroon. Turn over a rock,
and what looks like a bonanza of three or four
brightly coloured species becomes but one species
upon closer inspection.

NATURAL HISTORY

When there isn't much else around, good old
A. pilosa is always there to make your day. It spawns

year-round and has got to be our most common nudibranch of rocky shores. In Europe there are two spawning peaks, spring and autumn, and the life span is probably less that two years. In Nova Scotia, it spawns at least from March through November. It preys upon a variety of encrusting bryozoans such as *Alcyonidium*, *Flustrellidra,* and *Cryptosula* and occurs from the intertidal to depths of 170 metres.

DISTRIBUTION

In Europe from the Atlantic coast of Morocco north into the Baltic Sea, Iceland, and Greenland. Nova Scotia to Virginia, and on the Pacific coast from Aleutian Islands to Vancouver Island. In Atlantic Canada, reported from Nova Scotia and should eventually turn up everywhere.

COMMENTS

Acanthodoris pilosa provides food for thought. No animal should have so many options for its basic body colour. This is not the usual simple matter of the presence or absence of spots or stripes, or a matter of darker or paler—this is total colour differences. If the basis is genetic, then *A. pilosa* is remarkable to possess genes that turn out an entirely yellow or grey or maroon body. And what triggers these colour switches? If due to diet, which is true for many organisms including flamingos, then are the different species of bryozoan prey chemically responsible? But by what mechanism?

On the Bay of Fundy shore of Kings County, Nova Scotia, all colour varieties are found, whereas in adjacent Minas Basin specimens are either mauve or white, based on records from the 1960s–1980s.

Those observations suggest a dietary or other environmental influence, which is not unreasonable or unexpected, because Minas Basin is, in an environmental sense, a different world from Bay of Fundy. Perhaps the chemistry of whichever prey species is seasonally available to the planktonic veliger larvae may determine the colour.

Note: *Acanthodoris pilosa* is an equal opportunity research employer with opportunities for well-considered hypotheses and substantial operating grants.

Acanthodoris subquadrata

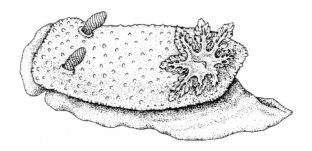

Order: **Nudibranchia**
Suborder: Doridacea
Family: Onchidorididae
Genus: Acanthodoris
Species: subquadrata
Authority: (Alder & Hancock, 1845)

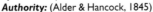

DESCRIPTION

To 25 mm, but this species is so rare that its maximum
size is unknown. Body is high and steep sided, with a
mantle cover that seems too small and perches on
top of the block-like body. Mantle surface has
many small conical papillae. Basal rhinophore
sheath is smooth edged, and the rhinophores are
tilted backwards. From above, the head and foot
margins project beyond the small mantle. Mid-rib of
each gill is fused to the mantle along half its length,
and thus the circlet of gills is always expanded. Tail
is short and broad with a slight middorsal crest.
As Alder and Hancock noted in 1845, the anatomy
is intermediate between that of *Acanthodoris* and
Goniodoris. Overall colour is yellowish mauve, with
pale yellow rhinophores.

NATURAL HISTORY

First dredged from "deepish water" at Torbay, England, it was presumed to be a subtidal species. However, one British and our one Nova Scotia report are from intertidal collection sites. Nothing is known of its life history and habits.

DISTRIBUTION

If appears that only seven specimens of *A. subquadrata* have ever been recorded, and two of those, the 1864 and 1966 specimens, have not previously been publicized. The records are:

England
- Torbay, Devon, May 1845, 1 specimen
- Mouth of the Dee, Merseyside, April 1851, 1 specimen
- Weymouth, Dorset, March 1864, 1 specimen
- Holy Island, Northumberland, 1908, 1 specimen

Northern Ireland
- Greenisland, County Antrim, 1944, 2 specimens

Nova Scotia
- Black Rock, Kings County, October 1966, 1 specimen

COMMENTS

How can I comment upon a species that no longer exists? In 1984, Thompson and Brown wrote (p. 64) "in our opinion these four are probably all simply damaged or parasitized specimens of *A. pilosa*." On that basis they concluded that *subquadrata* is synonymous with *pilosa*. They overlooked a fifth specimen, the 1851 report, which Alder and Hancock included in an appendix under item 7 *Doris subquadratus*.

Unfortunately, Thompson and Brown were not aware of the Nova Scotia specimen, which was subsequently verified in 1968 by Henning Lemche of the Zoology Museum, Copenhagen. Nor was anyone aware of the finely penned notation at the foot of the *Doris subquadrata* page in my copy of the 1845–55 Alder and Hancock nudibranch monograph.

The slightly faded amber script states, "A Specimen of this Doris was thrown ashore at Weymouth on a SE Gale in March 1864: W.A.S." On another page is a note stating that *A. pilosa* is common at Weymouth, thus indicating that the previous owner of my copy, William Ayshford Sanford of Taunton (1818–1902), was familiar with both species.

In light of this new information, I think we should reinstate *subquadrata*. It is probably "rare," because of a preference for deep water and because in a mixed collection of under-rock dorids it could easily get lost in that crowd of look-alikes. That accidental damage or parasitic infection could produce a consistent *subquadrata* body shape in England, Ireland, and Nova Scotia from 1845 to 1966 is more a specious argument than a species one.

Adalaria proxima

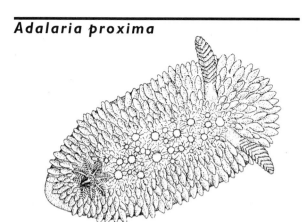

Order: **Nudibranchia**
Suborder: Doridacea
Family: Onchidorididae
Genus: Adalaria
Species: proxima
Authority: (Alder & Hancock, 1854)

DESCRIPTION

To 25 mm, but usually less than 17 mm. Body usually
pale yellow with darker rhinophores but can be
entirely white. Mantle bears numerous short, stiff,
stalked bulbous tubercles, many of which taper to a
cone-shaped tip. In the middorsal region, many of
the large spicule rods embedded in the mantle radi-
ate from the bases of the largest tubercles in a
sunburst pattern. The posterior gap in the circlet
of gills is filled in by a long anal papilla. Each simple
pinnate gill is located in a separate pit.

NATURAL HISTORY

This species and *Onchidoris muricata* are two of the
most common and widely distributed intertidal (and
subtidal to 60 m) dorid nudibranchs on the boreo-
arctic coasts of Europe and North America. Both

species prey upon encrusting colonies of bryozoans, especially *Electra pilosa*, and the bryozoans grow on rocks, piers, floating docks, small rockweeds, and large kelp. Both dorid species vary from white to yellow, both eat the same food at the same place at the same time, and both spawn from February to May and then expire at age 9 to 10 months. Consequently only tiny juveniles make up the population in summer.

The larva of *A. proxima* differs fundamentally from that of *O. muricata*. The latter has an old-fashioned, basic planktotrophic larva that drifts about for 50 to 60 days, whereas *A. proxima* is right up there with the fast crowd. It has the new, improved, supercharged, hi-tech lecithotrophic larva that risks its life in the dangerous plankton environment for only a few hours, or few days at most, before hitting the benthic big time and nine months of bacchanalian bryozoan banqueting.

DISTRIBUTION

A northern species reported from British Isles, Denmark, Norway, Iceland, Greenland, and south to southern New England states. On the west coast of North America from Bering Sea to California. On that coast it has three old aliases: *Adalaria pacifica*, *A. virescens*, and *A. albopapillosa*. In Atlantic Canada white dorids are known from all provinces, but until these specimens have their teeth examined, anyone who names them needs to have their head examined.

COMMENTS

Recently, a British Columbian opisthobranchologist, Dr. Sandra Millen, compared many Pacific and Atlantic species and discovered that several West Coast nudibranchs do not differ from their European counterparts. That was a bit of a shock, but she delved even deeper and discovered that the only reliable differences between the genera *Adalaria* and *Onchidoris* are in the shape and number of radular teeth. However, even these differences nearly overlap, and even more discouraging was the discovery that juvenile *Adalaria* have *Onchidoris*-type teeth until they reach 8 to 10 mm in body length. To have a species switch from one genus to another in mid-life is enough to reduce a taxonomist to tears.

Fortunately, at the same period in England three marine sluggers (Havenhand, Thorpe, and Todd) were equally frustrated by the fact that although *Adalaria* and *Onchidoris* are just about identical, their egg masses and type of larva are dramatically different. Those Brits didn't fool around; they compared 13 enzymes, coded by 14 loci, with the horizontal starch gel electrophoresis method. From their biochemical results, they learned that *Adalaria* is in the process of splitting off from its ancestral *Onchidoris* stock and has altered a few genes thus far, but not enough that it shows with a mantle on. The big gene split is in reproductive strategy towards lecithotrophy, but even that is not complete, because *Adalaria* can feed as larvae and/or use their yolk reserves. All true lecithotrophic larvae have sacrificed that feeding option. Thus, what we are witnessing is a new genus taking its first evolutionary steps.

Onchidoris muricata

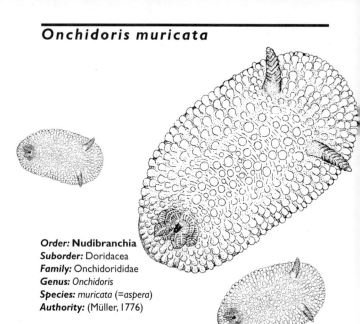

Order: **Nudibranchia**
Suborder: Doridacea
Family: Onchidorididae
Genus: Onchidoris
Species: muricata (=aspera)
Authority: (Müller, 1776)

DESCRIPTION

To 14 mm, but much smaller in late summer and autumn. Body colour varies from brilliant crystalline white to pale creamy yellow. Mantle bears numerous stalked, nearly flat-topped tubercles, packed with long spicules that may project from the surface. On the dorsum, large spicule rods run transversely and are densely packed in parallel. As previously discussed, this species and *Adalaria proxima* are often indistinguishable. There are reliable radular tooth differences, but these apply only to individuals in excess of 10 mm body length.

NATURAL HISTORY

The natural history account under *Adalaria proxima* is equally applicable here. The greatest difference lies in their spawn, for an *O. muricata* egg mass may have over 50,000 small eggs, whereas *A. proxima* spawn may contain only 2,000 large eggs. Towards the end of spawning, this dorid ceases feeding, and its gut tract atrophies and is converted into the final batch of gametes before death from starvation.

The shelled, planktonic veliger larvae drift in search of bryozoans and cannot metamorphose into shell-less sea slugs until they settle upon the likes of an *Electra pilosa* or *Membranipora membranacea* colony. Some mysterious chemical signal from their bryozoan prey triggers changes in the behaviour and anatomy of the molluscan larvae: they cease swimming, they shed their tiny coiled shell, they enlarge their foot for crawling, they change from cilia feeding to rasping and sucking, and thus they become slugs. Without that biochemical bryozoan elixir they would all die as larvae.

Although *Onchidoris muricata* is a cold-water dorid, at the southern limits of its range with a drifting larval period of as much as 50 to 60 days, the young become widely dispersed by ocean currents, even into lethal environments. The larvae may settle and survive for a few months in spring, but with the onset of warm summer sea temperatures they die off. This dispersal phenomenon is significant information for slug watchers, for it indicates that you never know what may show up from these unpredictable infusions of invisible larvae. You should examine your favourite slug sites every year, because there may well be a surprise species newly ensconced.

DISTRIBUTION

In Europe from northern France and British Isles to Arctic Russia, Iceland, Greenland, and then south to Connecticut. On the Pacific coast from Alaska to California, where it was also known as *O. hystricina* and *O. varians*. Probably common throughout Atlantic Canada.

COMMENTS

In most nudibranch groups it is only the species that may be difficult to tell apart, but within the dorid family this problem is elevated to the level of genus. Even the experts often feel unsafe in this quagmire, but as more and more nudibranch specialists come on stream, there is hope of a light at the end of the tunnel, at some point in time.

Not only may we expect additional European genera to be found in Atlantic Canada, but there may be new endemic genera as well—which also means, of course, new undescribed species. Those possibilities aside, there is still plenty of scope just deciphering our present dorid fauna.

I have seen and photographed several "peculiar" specimens that might fit into *Onchidoris*. Note that we have but two species of that genus recorded from Atlantic Canada, whereas in Europe these same two may be accompanied by *Onchidoris depressa, inconspicua, oblongata, pusilla,* or *sparsa*. Do we or don't we have those species on this side of the Atlantic? Another treatise looking for an author.

Not only are these dorid nudibranchs cause for taxonomic consternation within their own family, they have been equally devastating to bryozoan classification experts. Those experts recognize several species within the bryozoan genus *Membranipora,* and two of those species have spiny surfaces. In 1984, Harvell demonstrated that when *O. muricata* attacked colonies of the unspined *Membranipora membranacea,* within two days a protective deterrent of spines grew up from the bryozoan colony. These spines become permanent embellishments, and thus, within a mere 48 hours, the colony changes to another "species." It is obvious that these bryozoans are smarter than the taxonomists trying to understand them. These little creatures have found a shortcut to apparent speciation. "After all," they are heard to reason, "why invest all that energy in growing spines when there is a good possibility that those dastardly dorids may not even find us!"

Onchidoris bilamellata

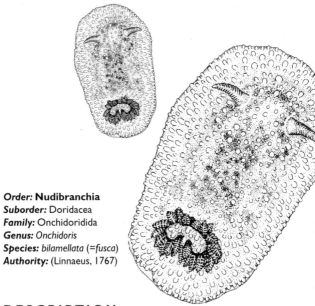

Order: **Nudibranchia**
Suborder: Doridacea
Family: Onchidorida
Genus: Onchidoris
Species: bilamellata (=fusca)
Authority: (Linnaeus, 1767)

DESCRIPTION

To 40 mm, but usually 15 to 30 mm. Body a dull
white, mottled with patches of light and dark brown
pigment, these often forming a rectangular pattern
from rhinophores to gills. Circlet of 16 to 32 simple
pinnate gills enclose the anal papilla and several
tubercles. Mantle surface bears numerous short,
club-shaped tubercles stiffened by elongate calcareous spicules. Similar spicules occur throughout the
mantle.

NATURAL HISTORY

Most dorid nudibranchs live under rocks and eat
soft prey. *Onchidoris bilamellata* lives under rocks
intertidally in Europe and North America and is
usually abundant. Although well known since first
described in 1767 by the great Linnaeus himself, it

was not until 1954 that two biologists (Barnes and Powell) discovered what this nudibranch had discovered millions of years previously. It is possible to live under a rock and yet avoid having to eat all those yukky, slimy, poisonous sponges, bryozoans, and cnidarians. Just wait for the flood tide, and then crawl up and onto the exposed rock surface and feast on the gourmet "crab meat" of barnacles. Barnacles are sessile crustaceans living in white cone-shaped "crab shells" cemented to hard surfaces. There is an unlimited supply of intertidal barnacles, and the slug feeds by perching atop the barnacle and ripping off its valve cover through a suspected combination of rasping, pushing, and biochemical means. Once the barnacle's soft parts are exposed, the nudibranch employs its very special, bulbous buccal pump and sucks them out, leaving behind the many bristly crustacean legs and other indigestibles. With a fibre optics probe, it might be possible to produce a documentary film of this entry from *inside* the barnacle fortress.

This sea slug's life history commitment to barnacles is unique among nudibranchs, and it is total. Juvenile and adult *O. bilamellata* eat only barnacles. In early summer, barnacle spat settles on rocks, and the sea slugs are never far behind. The dorid veliger larvae have, in fact, been swimming about as plankton for the previous 70 to 80 days, feeding on phytoplankton and trying to avoid the ignominious fate of being seized by an adult barnacle and eaten, while at the same time trying to grow large enough to successfully attack the youngest barnacles. The juvenile nudibranchs feast upon barnacle meat through summer, autumn, and into winter, and by January they are large enough to commence spawning, which they do from late January into April. The egg masses are attached to sides and undersides of rocks and may contain over 100,000 ova, all enclosed in a white gelatinous ribbon deposited by the dorid in a beautiful pattern of loops arranged in concentric circles. The eggs hatch in four to six weeks, depending upon temperature.

The adults spawn themselves to death, literally. When they exhaust their stored energy reserves for gamete production, they switch to a process termed autolysis (self-digestion) and turn their own internal organs into more eggs and sperm. By April or May nearly every adult has self-destructed. Note that this is not a conspicuous summer species, so look for it from October to April.

DISTRIBUTION

In Europe from France to White Sea of Russia, then Iceland, Greenland, and south to Connecticut. On the Pacific coast from Alaska to Mexico. Primarily intertidal to 20 m. In Atlantic Canada reported from Newfoundland, Nova Scotia, and New Brunswick. Often rare in collections simply because most fieldwork in Atlantic Canada is a summer activity, a period when *O. bilamellata* is very small and very inconspicuous.

COMMENTS

Most gourmet diets are expensive, and even *Onchidoris bilamellata* has to pay, and the price is high. They have to saturate coastal waters with their planktonic larvae so that whenever there is a settlement of barnacle spat, the slug larvae are there to pounce. But, drifting about in the plankton as edible veliger larvae for two to three months is practically suicidal. Juvenile fish and crustaceans gorge themselves with veligers. Therefore, to compensate for such incredible losses, the adults eat and eat, grow large, and then in frigid February spawn with everything they've got, converting their body tissues and ending their lives as shrunken husks within a year of their birth.

Each of the few millions of larvae that do make it to juvenilehood ends up sitting atop the razor-sharp crown of a barnacle cone. Looking like a miniature scoop of chocolate-chip ice cream in a hard cone, it presents a tempting, bite-size morsel for fish cruising over the intertidal at high water. However, if there is one thing that fish abhor it is an acid taste in their mouths. All acidic morsels are vigorously spat back out. Somehow, *O. bilamellata* knows this and will nonchalantly munch on its lunch all exposed to the jaws of death, knowing that its skin will pump out free sulphuric acid (from pH 2 to 1) all over anything that dares interrupt its gourmet repast.

Are you wondering how an animal can make, store, and release sulphuric acid from its skin without itself going up in smoke? Well, so am I.

Issena pacifica

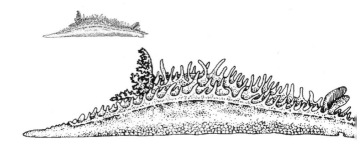

Order: **Nudibranchia**
Suborder: Doridacea
Family: Triophidae
Genus: Issena (=*Colga*)
Species: pacifica
Authority: (Bergh, 1894)

DESCRIPTION

To 65 mm. Narrow mantle is covered with numerous papillae of various lengths. Mantle edge has about 100 papillae. General body colour is yellowish white except where reddish brown viscera show through. Up to seven tripinnate gills, behind which is the anal papilla.

NATURAL HISTORY

Typically reported from depths of 80 to 130 fathoms: yes, fathoms not metres. Off Greenland, in the same dredged material were tunicates, crinoids, and hydroids, which is not very informative. Off Halifax, the story is more interesting, because that particular deepwater site (50 to 60 fathoms) has been sampled several times. Across the soft sediments in that area are scattered many rocks on which grow pink "cauliflowers," which most probably are the prey of *Issena pacifica*. The "cauliflowers" that make up this underwater garden are actually colonial coral animals. The species is *Duva multiflora* Verrill, a soft coral related to tropical forms, and the stalked "cauliflower" heads are clusters of little eight-tentacled, anemone-like polyps. As you may imagine, the numerous cavities provided by the "cauliflower" heads are utilized as dens by other animals. In addition, there are other sessile and free-living creatures associated with the rocks, and thus far, over 60 invertebrate species have been identified in these little rock-garden communities.

DISTRIBUTION

First reported from Alaska, but found since in northern Europe, southern Greenland, off Cape Cod, Massachusetts, and off Nova Scotia near Halifax Harbour.

COMMENTS

This deepwater species is included because the story of why we have *Issena* nudibranchs and *Duva* corals in the Nova Scotia Museum's collections is worth relating.

A typical museum budget does not include the annual operating costs of an oceanographic research vessel. Were it not for the big bucks of geological explorations in the oceans, especially oil, gas, and minerals, we biologists would still be grabbing and guessing and gassing about what we imagine the animal communities of the deep sea actually look like. For several decades exploration companies have been photographing the sea bottom and then contracting biologists, in some cases an entire museum staff of invertebrate experts, to identify animals, tracks, holes, and even shadows of creatures. The geologists are, of course, hoping to discover useful correlations between different animal communities and different geological features and formations.

Once a towed camera is at the sea floor, it can collect hundreds and hundreds of records of species and habitats, whereas when a biologist's grab sampler hits bottom it grabs whatever is there and squeezes it all together. It may require half, or even a full, day to complete one grab, and if a large stone has prevented closure of the jaws most of the sample can wash out as the apparatus is winched in. Another limitation of grabs and dredges, and even nets, is their sampling inefficiency over rough rocky areas. Fortunately, if you are interested in how biologists analyse and interpret undersea photographs, there is a recent, excellent, nontechnical publication based on our own Atlantic Canada offshore explorations. It is listed in the References for Particular Species under Lawrence et al. and covers the continental shelf from southwest of Nova Scotia to east of Newfoundland. The colour photos of animal communities are remarkable revelations of life in the dark depths.

Palio dubia

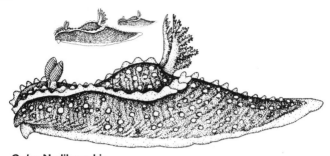

Order: **Nudibranchia**
Suborder: Doridacea
Family: Polyceridae
Genus: *Palio* (=*Polycera*)
Species: *dubia* (=*lessoni*)
Authority: (M. Sars, 1829)

DESCRIPTION

To 30 mm, but usually 10 to 15 mm. Body is always greenish (although *P. dubia* is not a plant eater) with a speckled yellow surface. Speckles are the yellow tips of short tubercles scattered over the body and arranged in a row around the edge of the mantle from the middorsal circlet of gills to the frontal margin. Tail has a middorsal row of yellow-tipped tubercles. Up to five tripinnate gills in the cluster and to each side a white, branching, fleshy tubercle.

NATURAL HISTORY

Polycera dubia is often found on the same rocks as *Ancula gibbosa* where, as everyone agrees, it is preying only upon the encrusting colonies of tiny bryozoans of phylum Ectoprocta. In England, one bryozoan genus, *Eucratea*, prodominates, but there probably are others because *P. dubia* occurs not only on rocks but also on leaves of eelgrass (*Zostera*), on blades of kelp (*Laminaria*), on large hydroids, and on old, encrusted mussel shells. On all such substrates, if examined closely, one can usually find epizoitic bryozoan colonies, which may be gelatinous, chitinous, or calcareous. From all this choice, the favourites of *P. dubia* have yet to be determined.

Connecticut seems to be the southern limit of *P. dubia,* and it is present only from March to June. If it cannot tolerate the warm summer temperatures, as suggested, then the annual infusion of larvae in March must come from populations in cooler waters either off the coast or perhaps from Bay of Fundy populations. In contrast, Nova Scotia reports of this species span the year from March to November. That three-month hiatus in winter collecting records is a widespread phenomenon in Atlantic Canada research reports and amply demonstrates that field biologists are capable of making intelligent decisions.

DISTRIBUTION

In Europe from France to the White Sea of Arctic Russia, then Iceland, Greenland, and south to Connecticut. In Atlantic Canada, *P. dubia* has been collected in Minas Basin, Annapolis Basin, and Digby, Lunenburg, and Guysborough counties.

COMMENTS

There is considerable historical evidence that *Palio dubia* and *P. nothus* have often been confused, and thus some of the information reported supposedly for the one may actually apply to the other. One particularly perplexing bit of information concerns their vertical distribution. In 1976, Thompson and Brown wrote that *P. dubia* occurred in intertidal pools in Europe. They did not mention *P. nothus* in that 1976 book. In 1984, the same authors wrote that *P. dubia* was sublittoral and found from depths of 10 to 100 metres, and that *P. nothus* is the species that occurs intertidally. However, in Connecticut and Nova Scotia *P. dubia* is found intertidally, and the rarity of *P. nothus* reports precludes any further discussion.

Palio nothus

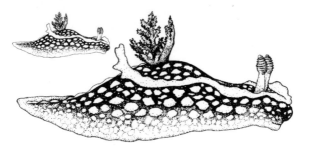

Order: **Nudibranchia**
Suborder: Doridacea
Family: Polyceridae
Genus: *Palio (=Polycera)*
Species: *nothus*
Authority: (Johnston, 1838)

DESCRIPTION

This species is very similar to *Palio dubia,* but
several authors have convinced themselves that they
differ as follows:

Palio dubia	*Palio nothus*
1. Where not pigmented, body is translucent white.	1. Where not pigmented, body is opaque white.
2. Tubercles are tall, yellow tipped.	2. Tubercles are short and white.
3. Tubercle shaft and base are same colour as body.	3. Tubercle shaft, base, and adjacent body area are white.
4. Rhinophores are slender.	4. Rhinophores stout.
5. It has up to 13 rhinophore lamellae.	5. It has up to 9 lamellae.
6. Radular teeth are slender.	6. Radular teeth are broad.

Item 5 must be taken with a grain of sea salt, because
smaller *dubia* have fewer lamellae, and there is one illustration of *nothus* in the literature with 11 lamellae on
one rhinophore and 9 on the other!

NATURAL HISTORY

Life history may be similar to *P. dubia*, as it is found on bryozoan-coated rocks, and in one report it consumed *Bowerbankia* while in captivity.

DISTRIBUTION

Because of past confusions with *P. dubia*, the real geographic distribution of *P. nothus* is unknown.

COMMENTS

There are no authenticated records for *P. nothus* in Atlantic Canada, but it must occur here, as there are reports from New England. Thompson and Brown (1984, p. 73) have verified photographs of both *Palio* species from New England, and Meyer's description (1971) of her "*P. dubia*" material from Nova Scotia and New England fits the criteria for *P. nothus* of nine or fewer rhinophoral lamellae. Meyer noted that Gould (1870) had counts of 12 and 13 lamellae in his Massachusetts specimens of *P. dubia*. Now we know that Gould was correct and that Meyer had a first for North America, but we are frustrated in not knowing whether Meyer's dissected specimens came from Nova Scotia or Maine or Massachusetts.

Actually, Meyer may not have had a first for North America, only a first for the western Atlantic. *Palio zosterae* on the west coast from British Columbia to California (see picture in Behrens, 1980) is the spittin' image of the European *P. nothus*, and the west coast species also loves to snack on *Bowerbankia* bryozoans. Looks like another thesis in search of a student.

Cadlina laevis

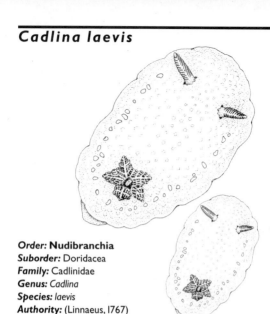

Order: **Nudibranchia**
Suborder: Doridacea
Family: Cadlinidae
Genus: *Cadlina*
Species: *laevis*
Authority: (Linnaeus, 1767)

DESCRIPTION

To 30 mm. A flattened, translucent white animal,
with a broad mantle skirt in which are embedded 20
or more lemon-yellow poison glands. Mantle surface
coated with small, soft tubercles.

NATURAL HISTORY

In Europe, this species is often locally common, at
and below the low intertidal along rocky and boulder
shores. *Cadlina laevis* preys upon slime sponges and
has a slimy, glistening, translucent quality that serves
as camouflage. Sponges such as *Halisarca* lack both
mineral and fibre skeleton and form a slimy yellow
coating on the undersides of rocks and on surfaces
of rock overhangs and ceilings of caverns. Energetic
rock rolling in tide pools may reveal this dorid slug,

but remember always to roll all rocks back to their original position and thereby restore, not destroy, that habitat.

C. laevis is one of those unusual molluscs that produce large eggs with enough nutrients that a planktonic larval period is unnecessary. From those eggs hatch miniature slugs. Time to hatching, even at 10° C, is about 50 days, yet there are still sufficient energy reserves within the livers of these juveniles to sustain them for that first critical week of their lives—that is, until they find a nice yummy patch of poisonous slime sponge.

In Europe, egg masses are recorded from August, September, November, February, and March.

DISTRIBUTION

Arctic Atlantic from Greenland to Massachusetts, and from Russia to Spain. From intertidal to depths of 800 m. All Atlantic Canada specimens are from the intertidal of the Minas Basin, but Bay of Fundy specimens are reported from Eastport, Maine.

COMMENTS

The reproductive strategies of Atlantic Canada's nudibranchs and sacoglossans will provide investigative material for many an amateur naturalist and many a student thesis, for years to come. Not one of the more than 40 species has had its life history elucidated. The challenge is that whereas most aquatic invertebrates employ but one of the three basic reproductive strategies and are genetically limited to that method, some of the opisthobranchs can easily switch from one strategy to another. We will never discover if any or how many of Atlantic Canada species have this ability until egg masses from every season of the year are investigated.

The three basic parental "do-what's-best-for-the-kids" strategies are founded on a sound ecological logic that goes something like this. Strategy 1: produce planktotrophic larvae. If the parents have eaten all the locally available food (e.g., all hydroid colonies), then the wise response is to lay small eggs that hatch quickly into planktonic larvae that drift and feed on phytoplankton for a few weeks, knowing that at least a small percentage will eventually stumble upon another hydroid McDonalds. Strategy 2: produce lecithotrophic larvae. If adequate food supplies are available for the kids locally, but these are scattered about in patches, then larger eggs are laid, and a short-lived larva (two to three days) is produced, which has a good chance of finding a local fast-food outlet before it dies of exhaustion. Strategy 3: go for direct development. If there is wall-to-wall food across the sea floor, the parents share it by laying large yolky eggs. The kids can then spend their entire larval life within the egg and hatch as miniature slugs right onto the banquet table and immediately pig out with their parents.

Several species of sea slugs seem to have all three software programs in their genetic files and can plug in whichever is appropriate to the current food supply situation. In Atlantic Canada, might a starving *Cadlina laevis* switch from number 3 to number 1 strategy? We just don't know.

Cadlina marginata

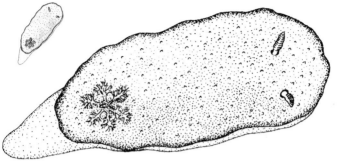

Order: Nudibranchia
Suborder: Doridacea
Family: Cadlinidae
Genus: Cadlina
Species: marginata (=luteomarginata)
Authority: MacFarland, 1905

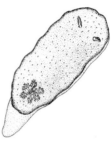

DESCRIPTION

To 35 mm. Similar to *C. laevis* except that the mantle margin and each of the small tubercles are yellow.

NATURAL HISTORY

On the west coast of North America, *Cadlina marginata* is reported to prey upon at least 10 species of sponges, including those with fibrous and siliceous spicules. *Cadlina laevis*, in contrast, avoids sponges with such skeletal supports and concentrates upon the amorphous slime sponges. Near San Diego, California, *C. marginata* was found not only on sponges beneath rocky overhangs but also on the sandy sea floor, feeding on an unusual sponge adapted to that habitat.

DISTRIBUTION

Until found on the west coast of Ireland by Lemche in 1971, this was considered a Pacific Ocean species, ranging from British Columbia to Baja, California. However, photographs taken underwater near Lunenburg, Nova Scotia, in 1973 are of *Cadlina marginata*, and additional specimens were found near Halifax.

COMMENTS

It is obvious that sponges are sitting ducks. They have no evident defence against ferocious jaws, but have you ever seen a sponge with great chunks bitten out? Not likely. Their defence is invisible chemicals, which are toxic, noxious, repugnant, distasteful, and other adjectives yet to be discovered.

But once again, our beautiful sea slugs demonstrate their superb understanding and mastery of biochemical interactions, for they consume the sponges and cleverly transfer the unadulterated toxins to special storage glands on the dorsal surface of their mantle cover and release these weapons whenever fish get too nosey.

Biochemists can tell you which species of sponge a *Cadlina* has recently eaten by identifying and tabulating the toxins in the skin of that slug. Such compounds as furan 20, pallescensin-A(16), dendrolasin (15), pleraplysillin-1(17), idiadione (19), isonitrile 23, isothiouyante 24, and furodysinin (18) provide the clues.

Dendronotus frondosus

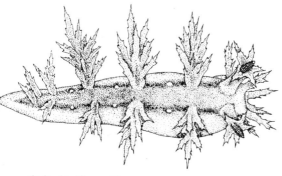

Order: Nudibranchia
Suborder: Dendronotacea
Family: Dendronotidae
Genus: *Dendronotus*
Species: *frondosus*
Authority: (Ascanius, 1774)

DESCRIPTION

To 100 mm, but usually 20 to 30 mm in intertidal zone. Easily recognized by the row of large, bushy (arborescent) cerata along each side of the body and similar but smaller branching processes on the rhinophore sheath and along the edge of the frontal veil.

This species comes in an amazing variety of colours and patterns, from white through yellow to brown, and may have contrasting stripes, bands, or spots. In general, it is pale until 4 mm in length and then acquires the vivid patterns. Beyond 30 mm in length it gradually fades to a uniformly pale grey or orange.

NATURAL HISTORY

This is a hydroid predator that switches its diet to different hydroid genera as it grows larger. This behaviour may help explain the progressive changes in body colour with age. In Nova Scotia, extreme low-water spring tides expose large pools where the Bear River flows into Annapolis Basin, and here all colour varieties of *D. frondosus* have been collected at the same time, including many 75-mm orange giants. These bushy orange beauties are a winner in a home marine aquarium tank.

The combined reports of spawning periods from North America and Europe indicate that this species reproduces from the coldest to the warmest seasons of the year. The egg mass is a round, gelatinous cushion in which a zigzag string of chalk-white eggs is folded back and forth, creating a complex pattern. Both planktotrophic and lecithotrophic larvae have been reported. It may be that *D. frondosus* has several life history strategies up its slimy sleeve, because researchers differ in their conclusions. Some report a life span of only three months, others of two years, and there are records of one generation and two generations per year.

DISTRIBUTION

Arctic regions south to Atlantic coast of France, to New Jersey, to California, and along the northern Asiatic coast. Common intertidally in Atlantic Canada.

COMMENTS

G. A. Robilliard has devoted more time studying this genus than anyone. He discovered several new species and had to redescribe older species more thoroughly. Combinations of colour, patterns, branching patterns of cerata, and width of foot help separate the various species, but tooth structure proved the most reliable diagnostic feature. He also discovered that in the Puget Sound area of Washington State (and this may be true of Atlantic Canada) *Dendronotus frondosus* occurs in four or five distinct colour and size morphs, each living and feeding in different habitats. This is textbook evolutionary speciation. Are we witnessing the breakup of *D. frondosus* from a generalist feeder into four or five specialist species? If so, they have a ways to go, because the tooth morphology of these populations is still identical.

Dendronotus dalli

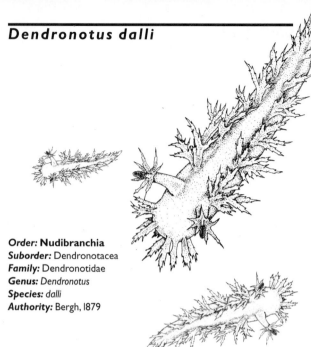

Order: **Nudibranchia**
Suborder: Dendronotacea
Family: Dendronotidae
Genus: *Dendronotus*
Species: *dalli*
Authority: Bergh, 1879

DESCRIPTION

To 135 mm. Similar to *D. frondosus* but usually white.
May be pearl pink or salmon pink on the West
Coast, but is pale orange in southeast Newfound-
land coastal waters.

NATURAL HISTORY

This is a species for scuba divers, because you start to
find it at depths of 12 m to 18 m, and it continues to at
least 110 m. Because *D. dalli* is so large and pale,
divers notice this species. Three 45-mm specimens
were gathered from a 14-m depth in Logy Bay, Newfoundland, in August 1970. It likes strong currents
and clings tenaciously to the hydroids growing there.
West Coast spawning reports are from January to
March and August to October, which suggests two
generations per year.

DISTRIBUTION

In the literature, this is a northeast Pacific Ocean nudibranch ranging from the Bering Straits south to Washington State. However, an east coast New England species *D. elegans* Verrill, 1880, is now believed to be identical, and examination of teeth from Nova Scotia and Newfoundland specimens proved they were *Dendronotus dalli*.

COMMENTS

It is peculiar that most references to this species concern individuals in the 40- to 60-mm size range. Where are all the juveniles? Are they a different colour or in a different area, or both?

In Atlantic Canada we have two large, pale orange, essentially identical bushy-backed slugs. If your specimen is from the intertidal or shallow water it probably is *Dendronotus frondosus*. If it is from depths greater than 18 m, it probably is *Dendronotus dalli*. Anything from in between needs its teeth examined, and this is where your handy, dandy, hobbyist's $60,000 scanning electron microscope comes in handy.

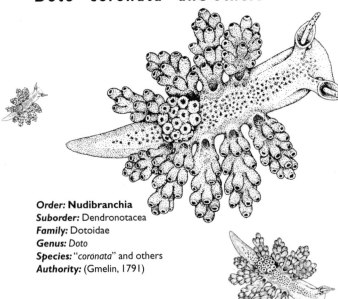

Order: Nudibranchia
Suborder: Dendronotacea
Family: Dotoidae
Genus: *Doto*
Species: "*coronata*" and others
Authority: (Gmelin, 1791)

DESCRIPTION

To 15 mm, but usually 4 to 7 mm. Easily recognized
by the rough, pineapple-shaped cerata, each tubercle
of which has a purplish red spot at the tip, and by the
distinctive pair of trumpet-shaped sheaths from which
the rhinophore tentacles protrude. Body is usually
cream colour with scattered red to purple flecks, but
may be quite dark or even white without any red
spots. If you do find any of these extreme "colour
varieties," you undoubtedly have an undescribed
species in your hand.

For over 100 years European malacologists considered *Doto coronata* to be a common species with
many colour variations. Recently, it has been discovered that many of those "varieties" are distinct species, often feeding on different species of hydroids,
laying differently shaped egg masses, spawning at

different times, found at different depths, and so on. Because "*coronata*" did not refer to just one species, it is not of much use any more, and we go back to square one and start the naming all over again. Thus there has been almost an explosion of species' descriptions in this genus. There are now at least 15 described species reported from the North Atlantic and at least 8 more waiting for names. The situation in Atlantic Canada in 1994 was:

1. *Doto onusta* Hesse, 1872: the common red- or purple-spotted species that is usually listed as *Doto coronata*.
2. *Doto* sp. A (of plate 13 in Just and Edmunds, 1985): similar to *onusta* but with very few red spots on very elongate cerata.
3. *Doto* sp. nov.: undescribed species, similar to species 1 and 2 above but with clusters of white spots forming a band around each tubercle, a wavy margin on the rhinophore sheath, and a pair of tiny cerata just behind the rhinophores.
4. *Doto* sp. nov.: undescribed white species, translucent to transparent with white flecks on the cerata and around the flared lip of the rhinophore sheath; the only other colour is from the creamy gonads and gut tract, which are visible through the transparent body.

NATURAL HISTORY

This complex of species preys upon many species of hydroids. In Atlantic Canada *Doto* slugs occur on both small and large colonies of hydroids, which in turn can be found attached to rocks, mussel shells, floats and mooring chains, floating docks, wharf pilings, and boat hulls and on the surface of large kelp blades. *Doto* species are quite inconspicuous in a tangle of hydroid branches, but their beautiful white ribbons of eggs will clue you to the presence of adults.

In Atlantic Canada, this genus has been collected from June through November with spawn found in June, July, and August. However, as we now know that at least four species are involved, it may be that some of these are winter or spring breeders, so we should not be surprised to eventually find adults and spawn throughout the year.

DISTRIBUTION

A worldwide genus of many species, and thus far reported from several localities in Nova Scotia, New Brunswick, and Newfoundland.

COMMENTS

This expanding complexity of *Doto* species can only be sorted out over a long time frame through patient collecting, accumulation of excellent macrophotographs of adults and egg masses, species identification of their hydroid prey, and ultimately the examination of the radular teeth by scanning electron microscope. For such reasons (among others) are provincial and national museums invaluable, for only at such centres can one expect to find a responsible repository for the permanent storage of specimens, photos, and data, be they geological, cultural, or biological. There, the gradual accumulation of information, often over several decades, will eventually constitute a size suitable for critical analysis. Only at that stage can new information be added to that general vital pool of humanity's accumulated knowledge.

Coryphella verrucosa

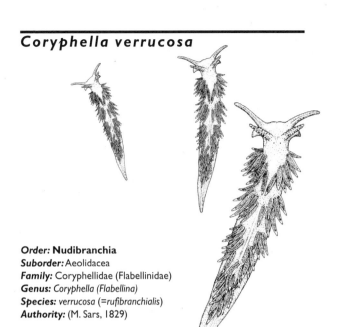

Order: **Nudibranchia**
Suborder: Aeolidacea
Family: Coryphellidae (Flabellinidae)
Genus: *Coryphella (Flabellina)*
Species: *verrucosa* (=*rufibranchialis*)
Authority: (M. Sars, 1829)

DESCRIPTION

Often 20 to 35 mm in length. Body long, translucent
white with five to seven clusters of cerata along each
side. Cerata reddish brown, maroon, or even tan,
but with brilliant white pointed tips. A middorsal
white stripe from heart to tip of tail, and a white
streak on upper surface of rhinophore and oral tentacles. Rhinophores have a rough, bumpy surface.
The lateral foot extension is but half the width of
the foot.

The five rather similar species of *Coryphella* reported from Atlantic Canada can be distinguished
with some confidence using the diagrams in Figure 4
(p.116). The relative position of the anus is important, as is the arrangement of the cerata on the
notum. The latter is the long, dorso-lateral, shelf-like
body extension on which the cerata are positioned.

This shelf may be wide or narrow, and between the cerata clusters it may be continuous, reduced, or absent.

In *C. verrucosa*, the notum ridge is absent between the clusters of cerata, and the anus is located just beneath the third row of cerata within the second ceratal cluster.

NATURAL HISTORY

This is the most common species, found intertidally and to depths of over 400 m on rocky substrates and feeding primarily upon hydroid species of the genus *Tubularia*. Spawning extends from March through late summer; adults then die, and juveniles grow throughout the winter. Thus, this is an annual life cycle.

DISTRIBUTION

A northern species, from the British Isles, Norway, Iceland, and Greenland south to Gulf of Maine. In Pacific area, from British Columbia and coast of Russia. Probably common throughout Atlantic Canada, but because of confusion in the past with other coryphellid species we really need to start all over again.

COMMENTS

After 160 years of usage, the name *Coryphella* has recently been changed to *Flabellina*. Neverthelesss, I have opted to defy the international "rules" and have retained the old name in this book, because 99.9 per cent of the literature concerning this common species will be listed under the name *Coryphella*. It will probably take another 10 years to thoroughly establish this new generic designation.

This particular species has been the most misidentified nudibranch in North America and Europe. Not until Kuzirian concentrated on this group for over four years, and in that time examined most of the old museum specimens and studied their radular teeth, did we finally obtain the clues that enabled us to separate the disparate shapes and colour forms into true species. The most reliable feature is tooth shape. The three rows of teeth on the radular ribbon consist of a central series of heavy serrated teeth and to each side a row of smaller triangular teeth. Figure 5 (p.126) illustrates the considerable and consistent differences among our local species.

Are you wondering why it would take four years to sort out four of these species? For an answer read Kuzirian's 22-page paper with its 89 literature references and gain an insight into the ramifications of such a seemingly simple marine biology project. What appeared to be a Mount Martock challenge became a Mount Everest test of perseverance. This is why professors surround themselves with keen, competent, naive graduate students: the profs operate base camps while their unsuspecting students are sent forth to conquer mountains.

FIG. 4 Pictorial Key to Five Species of Coryphella

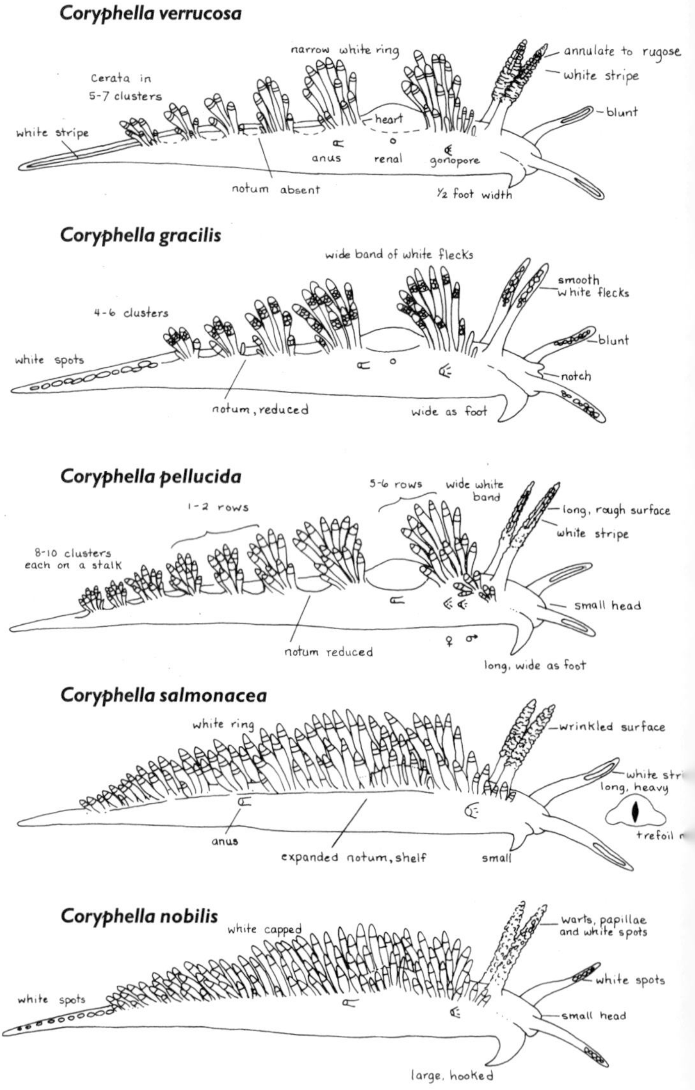

Coryphella verrucosa

- annulate to rugose
- white stripe
- blunt
- narrow white ring
- Cerata in 5-7 clusters
- heart
- anus
- renal
- gonopore
- white stripe
- notum absent
- ½ foot width

Coryphella gracilis

- wide band of white flecks
- smooth white flecks
- blunt
- notch
- 4-6 clusters
- white spots
- notum, reduced
- wide as foot

Coryphella pellucida

- 5-6 rows
- wide white band
- long, rough surface
- white stripe
- 1-2 rows
- 8-10 clusters each on a stalk
- small head
- notum reduced
- ♀ ♂
- long, wide as foot

Coryphella salmonacea

- white ring
- wrinkled surface
- white stripe
- long, heavy
- trefoil
- anus
- expanded notum, shelf
- small

Coryphella nobilis

- white capped
- warts, papillae and white spots
- white spots
- small head
- white spots
- large, hooked

116

Several subtle diagnostic features become more evident as you compare the same structure in each diagram.

1. *Shape and relative length of the anterior lateral foot extension*

2. *Relative position of the anus on the right side of the body*

3. *Relationship of the cerata (clustered, stalked, continuous) to the lateral notum shelf from which they originate*

4. *Surface texture and pigment pattern of the tentacles*

5. *Arrangement of white pigment at tips of the cerata*

6. *Amount of white pigment on the upper tail surface*

General body colour is not a reliable feature, because it varies according to the hydroid prey just consumed, which is visible through the transparent cerata. Also, if the large cream-coloured gonads are absent or reduced, the animals have an overall translucent or even transparent appearance.

Coryphella gracilis

Order: Nudibranchia
Suborder: Aeolidacea
Family: Coryphellidae
Genus: Coryphella
Species: gracilis (=stellata)
Authority: (Alder & Hancock, 1844)

DESCRIPTION

To 12 mm and similar to *C. verrucosa*, but the white
streak on tentacles is made up of scattered flecks
and on the body is limited to the tip of the tail. The
head has an anterior notch when viewed from above,
the oral tentacles are broad at their bases, and the
notum has four to six pairs of cerata clusters.
Between clusters the notum is present but reduced
in width. The anus is always just beneath the first
row of cerata in the second cluster. Cerata colour is
orange to crimson. The lateral foot extension is as
long as foot is wide.

NATURAL HISTORY

From the intertidal to at least 33 m, and a specialist
predator on *Eudendrium* hydroids. Spawning occurs in
late autumn and in early spring, and planktotrophic

larvae are produced, which swim for six to eight weeks. Thus there are at least two generations per year.

DISTRIBUTION

Reported from France, British Isles, Denmark, Iceland, and from Nova Scotia to Cape Cod, Massachusetts. Many old reports of *C. verrucosa* could well be *gracilis,* but without the actual specimens available for tooth comparisons we will never know.

COMMENTS

Hopefully from now on, with this new coryphellid criteria available, biologists will be able to get their species IDs correct the first time. So, as far as which coryphellids are where, it is back to square one, and counting.

Coryphella pellucida

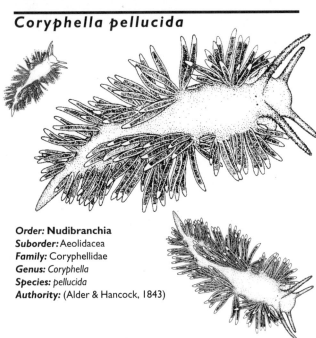

Order: **Nudibranchia**
Suborder: Aeolidacea
Family: Coryphellidae
Genus: *Coryphella*
Species: *pellucida*
Authority: (Alder & Hancock, 1843)

DESCRIPTION

To 30 mm. Body long, high, translucent white with
8 to 10 clusters of crimson-red, white-capped cerata.
The first cerata group has five to six diagonal rows,
while other clusters have but one or two rows. The
notum ridge is reduced between clusters, and thus each
row or cluster appears to be elevated on a common
stalk or pedicle. Rhinophores have a rough surface
and are longer than oral tentacles. Both pairs of tentacles have a dorsal white stripe. Foot extension is as
wide as foot and tapers to an acute point.

Anus is located in the gap between the first two
clusters of cerata. Beneath the first cerata cluster
are two genital openings, not the usual single combined gonopore. The anterior orifice is the male.

NATURAL HISTORY

This species is found on rocky substrates from shallows to 120 m where it concentrates on species of the hydroid genus *Eudendrium*, and of course it also nibbles on *Tubularia* in season. Spawning occurs from April into June, and juveniles are found from late July to November, indicating an annual life cycle.

DISTRIBUTION

France, British Isles, Norway, and Bay of Fundy to Cape Cod, Massachusetts. *Coryphella pellucida* should occur throughout Atlantic Canada, but Canadian reports are nearly as scarce as slug's feathers (a marine correlative for hen's teeth). Only the Minas Basin has reported in so far.

COMMENTS

None, until some unsuspecting, starry-eyed, graduate student is conned into a thesis project.

Coryphella salmonacea

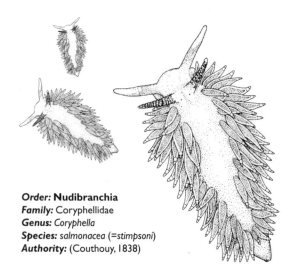

Order: **Nudibranchia**
Family: Coryphellidae
Genus: *Coryphella*
Species: *salmonacea* (=*stimpsoni*)
Authority: (Couthouy, 1838)

DESCRIPTION

To 40 mm. Body low, wide, opaque white with numerous, evenly spaced cerata arranged in two longitudinal bands on an expanded notum. Cerata are largest medially and smallest laterally, are orange-tan to reddish brown, and have a subapical white ring. All head tentacles are stout with a distal white patch. Oral tentacles are longer than the rhinophores, and the latter are often tan in colour and have a distinctive wrinkled surface. From the ventral aspect, the mouth region differs from other coryphellids in having a large, rounded extension to each side, creating a trefoil configuration. The anus is located about three-quarters posteriorly beneath the notum on the right side. The lateral foot extensions are small and set back from the anterior foot margin, as opposed to originating at the anterior foot corners.

NATURAL HISTORY

This species differs not only in morphology but also in life history and prey preference. Spawning occurs during the cold-water period of December to March, and the eggs of *C. salmonacea* are laden with yolk. After 25 to 52 days (varies with temperature of the water) juveniles hatch directly: there is no larval stage in this life history. The juveniles subsist upon the abundant *Tubularia* hydroids of summer, then switch to a most unusual diet of tunicates. The latter are sessile invertebrates, which are rather closely related to fish, but which secrete an outer case, the tunic, of plant-like cellulose. This coryphellid's special prey and egg-laying substrate is the colonial tunicate *Amaroucium*. The tiny tunicates live embedded in an inconspicuous, translucent brown to greyish, rather firm gelatinous tunic sheet that grows and spreads over rock surfaces and up the stalks of any algae or sessile animals with which it comes in contact. *Amaroucium* is a sort of science fiction "shapeless blob" that assumes the shape of whatever it engulfs.

DISTRIBUTION

Intertidal to a depth of over 600 m. Northern Norway, Iceland, Greenland, and south into Bay of Fundy and Gulf of Maine. Atlantic Canada reports are limited so far to Nova Scotia's Halifax, Digby, and Kings counties, and to St. Andrews, New Brunswick.

COMMENTS

Check out the revised edition of this guide in 10 years' time.

Coryphella nobilis

Order: **Nudibranchia**
Suborder: Aeolidacea
Family: Coryphellidae
Genus: *Coryphella*
Species: *nobilis*
Authority: Verrill, 1880
(*and* an undescribed **Species**)

DESCRIPTION

A large coryphellid to 50 mm in length with a long, high, translucent white body on which are two bands of maroon to reddish brown, tightly packed cerata along the notal brim. Cerata have a terminal white cap. White pigment flecks form a streak just posterior to the heart, along entire length of tail, and on the extremities of the tentacles. Head is relatively small. Rhinophore tentacles are usually tan and have a peculiar surface texture of minute warts and papillae. Anus is less than half way posterior and is high up near notum. Lateral foot extension is as long as foot width and usually hooked.

NATURAL HISTORY

As it has never been found in water less than 20 m deep, here is a species for scuba sluggers. It frequents rocky sea floors, where large hydroids of the genera *Sertularia* and *Halecium* abound. Spawning takes place during our "warm-water" season of late spring through summer, and planktotrophic larvae hatch. As with many other aeolid nudibranchs, the juveniles plunder the abundant summer crop of *Tubularia* hydroids.

DISTRIBUTION

Northern Norway, Iceland, Greenland, and New England, but no authenticated records from Atlantic Canada—yet.

COMMENTS

There is an additional deepwater *Coryphella* species found below 20 m and recognized by Kuzirian in his 1979 paper but as yet unnamed. It differs in living on soft sands and silts, where it preys upon a peculiar, large (10 cm high) solitary hydroid, *Corymorpha pendula,* which looks like a flower and even has root-like filaments that anchor its stalk in the soft sediments. The nudibranch has two generations per year and lays unique eggs for a coryphellid: there are multiple eggs per capsule. In Maine, New Hampshire, and Massachusetts adults and spawn of *C. sp.* were found in May, June, and August.

A 15-mm specimen of this new species and its *Corymorpha* prey were found on the sand flats of Scots Bay, Kings County, Nova Scotia, during an extremely low minus tide on 2 August 1977. The student collectors were strolling about on the sea floor, not scuba diving, which once again demonstrates the exciting potential of that fleeting but revealing hour that straddles an extreme low tide.

FIG. 5 Radular Teeth of Five Species of Coryphella

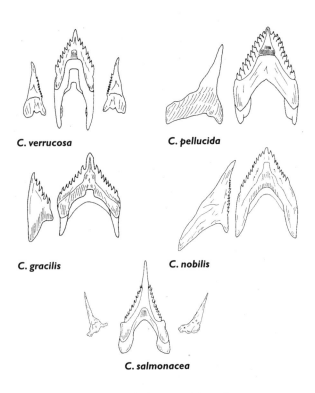

C. verrucosa

C. pellucida

C. gracilis

C. nobilis

C. salmonacea

In this genus there are only three teeth in each transverse row of teeth on the radular tongue: a large central saw-edged tooth and a lateral tooth to each side. (One lateral tooth has been omitted in drawings 2, 3, and 4.) The total number of rows of teeth on the rasping radula varies from an average of 12 rows in *verrucosa* to 36 rows or more in *pellucida*. Note that the lateral teeth of *pellucida* lack the serrated edge found in other species. The lateral teeth of *salmonacea* are much smaller and are peculiar in that both the smooth-edged and the serrated-edged type can be found mixed together on the same radula.

Eubranchus exiguus

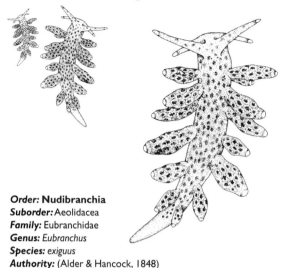

Order: Nudibranchia
Suborder: Aeolidacea
Family: Eubranchidae
Genus: *Eubranchus*
Species: *exiguus*
Authority: (Alder & Hancock, 1848)

DESCRIPTION

To 10 mm, but usually 4 to 6 mm. A translucent
yellowish brown slug with urn-shaped cerata spaced
well apart and often in pairs of one large and one
small ceras. Each ceras has two to three darker
bands of olive-brown flecks and one ring of white
flecks and terminates in a white nipple-shaped tip.
Two pair of tentacles with white tips and a band of
dark flecks in the mid-region. The curved anterior
foot margin lacks any projections.

NATURAL HISTORY

Often abundant on hydroid colonies that are in
turn growing on floating docks, old kelp blades, and
Zostera eelgrass. The slug's general body shape
closely resembles a portion of hydroid colony,
and this mimicry renders it nearly invisible.

However, numerous little white kidney-shaped egg masses attached to the hydroids immediately indicate that this aeolid is at home. If some of those egg masses seem definitely smaller than others, they probably belong to an even smaller nudibranch, *Tergipes tergipes*, often found in company with *E. exiguus*. These two species are representative of that category of voracious carnivores that can settle on hydroid colonies and eat them into oblivion within a few weeks, although it may take two or three quick generations of slugs to do so.

DISTRIBUTION

Europe and northeastern North America, including Nova Scotia, New Brunswick, and Newfoundland. This species will probably turn up everywhere in Atlantic Canada and become known as our most common and abundant aeolid.

COMMENTS

Most *Eubranchus* species have characteristically inflated cerata, flecks of colour on the body, and bands of flecks forming rings on both cerata and tentacles. The base colour and colour fleck patterns vary slightly from species to species (brownish, reddish, orangish, greenish, even colourless greyish), but several species have their own series of colour variations, some of which may closely resemble other species of *Eubranchus*, all of which makes this genus a real challenge—a real *headache* would be more appropriate terminology. Normally, examination of tooth morphology would settle the matter, but this complex of species has further confounded our quest after their true identity by possessing essentially identical teeth, a most unmolluscan condition. European experts now rely heavily upon a combination of colour pattern, food items, water depth, and habitat differences to separate their eight local species. There are about 24 species of *Eubranchus* worldwide. However, as you can now imagine, over the past 100 years the identification of eubranchid species has become one of confusion thrice compounded, such that many (dare we say most?) reports in the scientific literature simply are not the species that the poor author had convinced himself that they were.

In Atlantic Canada, there are at least the four species herein described, and peculiarly they may often be found together. From a collection of hydroids on a floating dock at St. Andrews, New Brunswick, there were *E. exiguus*, *E. olivaceus,* and several slugs 8 to 11 mm in length that closely resembled *E. rupium* (Möllek, 1842) of Europe. Obviously, colour macrophotography will be an essential tool for anyone attempting an analysis of this colourful genus in Atlantic Canada.

Eubranchus pallidus

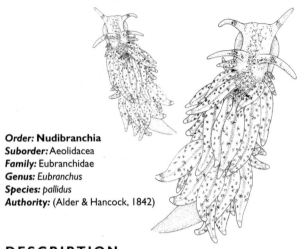

Order: **Nudibranchia**
Suborder: Aeolidacea
Family: Eubranchidae
Genus: *Eubranchus*
Species: *pallidus*
Authority: (Alder & Hancock, 1842)

DESCRIPTION

To 20 mm, but usually 8 to 10 mm. Has an overall
orange tint from the many orange flecks of pigment
scattered over the body and cerata, and occasionally
forming patches of orange on some body areas. The
two pair of tentacles have a dark pigment band in the
mid region, but the cerata lack the usual dark rings
found on most eubranchids. This species also differs
in that laterally there are many smaller cerata,
whereas medially they are large and inflated.

NATURAL HISTORY

In Europe this is considered an offshore species, not
a tide pool animal, and is usually collected by dredg-
ing. It reportedly feeds upon many species of
hydroids. The only verified Canadian record is a
9-mm specimen found on a rock during an extremely

low tide on 23 October 1976, at Cape Blomidon in Minas Basin, Nova Scotia. In 1964, Moore reported that it is "associated with hydroids, winter and spring; Bay of Fundy to Rhode Island," but he elaborated no further. Its life history on this side of the Atlantic is still unstudied.

It is worth noting that 1976 was a period of very high and very low tides, one of the peaks in an 18-year cycle, the next recurrence of which you just missed in 1994. In Minas Basin, such peak periods translate into 15- to 16-m tidal amplitudes, and at such times one does not have to dredge sea-bottom samples from aboard ship, for one can literally do a walk-about on the exposed seabed, sometimes for nearly half an hour before the tide turns and floods in again. Within the Bay of Fundy/Minas Basin system, these unusual tides provide unique opportunities for discovery and direct observation of rare and unusual creatures right in their natural deep-water habitats. Plan ahead for several summers on the Fundy Shore near the year 2012.

Of course snorkel diving and scuba diving for hydroid colony clusters might turn up more specimens of *Eubranchus pallidus*.

DISTRIBUTION

Commonly reported in Europe from Norway to the western Mediterranean, a few reports from southern New England, one from the Suez Canal, and only the one 1976 specimen from Atlantic Canada. Did you immediately think, after reading the previous sentence, "Only one specimen! Wow! Is that ever a rare species!"? Well, think again. You have it all wrong. Backwards actually. The thing that is rare in Atlantic Canada is persons who know how to find

E. pallidus. After all, distribution maps of marine animals are, if you're honest about it, simply maps of the distribution of the marine biologists who are chasing after those species.

COMMENTS

This is one of the few species of *Eubranchus* that can be verified by examination of the ribbon of teeth on the rasping radula. All eubranchids have three rows of teeth, and the teeth of the mid row are sturdy and strongly serrated, and look the same from species to species. The lateral teeth, in contrast, are simply flat thin plates with a projecting point on one side. In most species these plate teeth are long and narrow, but in *pallidus* they are quite short, about as high as they are long.

Eubranchus tricolor

Order: **Nudibranchia**
Suborder: Aeolidacea
Family: Eubranchidae
Genus: Eubranchus
Species: tricolor
Authority: Forbes, 1838

DESCRIPTION

To 30 mm. Of a uniformly greyish white colour with greatly inflated cerata. The only colour accents are the slight yellowish brown of the rhinophores, the opaque white caps of the cerata (on which there may be an additional narrow yellowish band), and visible within each transparent ceras a smooth brownish gut tract, which merges into an expanded violet area near its tip.

NATURAL HISTORY

In Europe this species is rarely found inter-tidally, but shows up frequently in bottom samples of shell gravels and stones to depths of 80 m.

Scuba divers at Eastport, Maine, found *E. tricolor* at 15 m on a rock and cobble substrate in a clump of the hydroid *Tubularia spectabilis*.

In Nova Scotia, small 5-mm individuals have been found intertidally in Minas Basin during extreme low-water tides, feeding on hydroids attached to stones. The hydroids in one collection were *Hydrallmania falcata*.

The combined Maine and Nova Scotia reports extend from May into November, and as *E. tricolor* appears to be a cold-water species, it is probably active throughout the year in Atlantic Canada as well as in our eastern Arctic waters. Diligent searching for *E. tricolor* along the coast of southern Maine has been unsuccessful, a situation very similar to the northern presence and southern absence of this species in France.

DISTRIBUTION

Until 1976, this sea slug was believed to be limited to Europe, from northern France to Norway and eastward into the White Sea of Arctic Russia. The specimens found in northern Maine in 1973 were the first to be officially reported from North America, although the first Nova Scotia specimen was collected in Minas Basin, 18 August 1970.

COMMENTS

In the standard reference for identification and distribution of all North American Atlantic coast marine invertebrates (Gosner, 1971) you will find *E. tricolor* listed. Yet, this was five years before *tricolor* was discovered in the western Atlantic. This mistake is rather complicated, resulting from Gosner (not a sea slug specialist) following the 1954 opinion of Pruvot-Fol (a sea slug expert) that *pallidus* is merely a colour variety of *tricolor* and, therefore, can only be referred to scientifically and nomenclaturally as *tricolor*. Thank goodness some of the experts also use terms such as "the greyish white species" and "the orange speckled species," because otherwise we might not know what they were writing about!

Eubranchus olivaceus

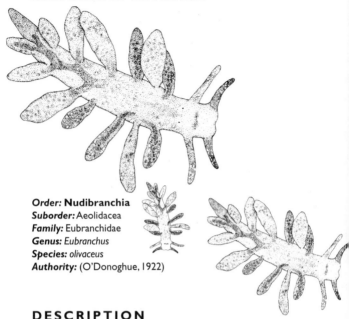

Order: **Nudibranchia**
Suborder: Aeolidacea
Family: Eubranchidae
Genus: *Eubranchus*
Species: *olivaceus*
Authority: (O'Donoghue, 1922)

DESCRIPTION

To 9 mm, more often 4 to 6 mm. Long slender body
and tail, translucent creamish body colour but with
an overall pale greenish tint due to the olive-green
extension of the gut tract within each ceras. The six
anterior cerata are aligned as three opposite pairs,
but the remainder are arranged alternately. Within
the posterior half of the body, the greenish gut tube
forms a conspicuous zigzag pattern, alternating from
the base of one ceras to the next. There are both
white and orange pigment flecks scattered sparsely
over body and cerata. Cerata are slender, but relatively large for the size of the animal, and are inflated
slightly about three-quarters distance from the base.
A ring of white flecks and one of orange flecks are
just discernable at this enlargement.

NATURAL HISTORY

Very little is known about this rare aeolid. Over a three-year period in Maine (1966–68) it was found feeding and spawning on the hydroid species *Obelia commisuralis* and *Campanularia flexuosa* from May through November.

In Atlantic Canada, specimens from New Brunswick and Nova Scotia were in miscellaneous mixes of unidentified (unfortunately) hydroids scraped off rocks, old kelp blades, and floating docks.

DISTRIBUTION

Eubranchus olivaceus was first discovered in 1922, on Vancouver Island, British Columbia, then reported from Washington State in the 1960s, and now is known as far south as Mexico. Nonetheless, these reports represent very few specimens, and *olivaceus* is today still considered a "very rare" West Coast sea slug. In 1966, this supposed West Coast nudibranch threw a surprise party in Maine by appearing in the collections of a sluggish graduate student. Since then *olivaceus* has been collected in company with other eubranchid species at St. Andrews, New Brunswick, and in Nova Scotia from East Ferry, Digby County, and at two localities in Minas Basin.

COMMENTS

Someday marine scientists and behavioural ecologists may wake up to the fact that this genus of animals, prior to speciation, neglected to read the official textbooks and especially those chapters that describe how each predator species must be a specialist and thusly avoid competition from similar species. Theoretically, if you do find several animal species preying upon the same food source, you should discover that each has developed different specialized mouth parts such that each predator species is feeding upon different parts of that food item, thus avoiding direct competition. This usually shows up elegantly in molluscs in the subtle differences in shape and size of the rasping radula and in tooth morphology, as one would predict.

The eubranchids are, therefore, most unusual for the different species have the same tooth morphology. Given this fact, one would predict that such similar species could avoid competition by each preying upon a separate hydroid species. In reality, these sea slugs seem to prefer partying together on whatever species of hydroids are available. Very often three or four species of *Eubranchus* are found together feeding and laying eggs on a hydroid colony. They may even be in company with *Tergipes tergipes,* a different genus of sea slug, which undermines the theoretical prediction even further. If all these predators were specialists attacking different parts of a hydroid colony, such as rhizomes, stalks, hydranths, or gonophores, then their teeth should differ, but they don't. The scientific consensus is that all these species are cropping only the meaty hydranth bodies, but does anyone really know for sure?

The theoretical implications and the research potential within the genus *Eubranchus* is evident. Here is an elegant, compact, functional model of multiple predators interacting with one another and with single prey species. The single prey species even varies over time, because a broad spectrum of hydroid genera and species are accepted by these carnivores.

An entire "community," for experimental purposes, could be maintained in a small jar. Predator generation turnover in eubranchids is in the order of four to six weeks with life spans of only four to six months. Energy input and transfer could be quantified and biomass determined. Each component in the system is readily subject to experimental manipulation. Presumably, a unique theoretical model could be generated, describing the energy equation(s) that perpetuate these mini-communities of voracious, nearly identical, predator species. They obviously aren't the least bit interested in pursuing the Darwinian laws of natural selection and taking the evolutionary path to niche specialization, thereby avoiding interspecific competition for food.

Cuthona gymnota

Order: **Nudibranchia**
Suborder: Aeolidacea
Family: Cuthonidae (Tergipedidae)
Genus: *Cuthona*
Species: *gymnota* (=*aurantia*)
Authority: (Couthouy, 1838)

DESCRIPTION

To 22 mm, but more often 6 to 12 mm. A pale cream
slug with diagonal rows of slender, finger-like, rosy-
orange cerata. The tips of these cerata are capped in
white, over which there usually is a subterminal orange
colour band. The head tentacles are without bands or
stripes; the oral tentacles are colourless, but the
translucent rhinophores have that rosy-orange tint.

NATURAL HISTORY

This beautiful nudibranch derives much of its colour
from the rose-pink-orange pigments of its prey,
those large hydroids of the genus *Tubularia*. There
are at least five species of *Tubularia* in Atlantic
Canada, and several of these are seasonal. *Cuthona
gymnota* simply switches from one species to another
with the changing seasons, and this is why spawn and

juveniles can be found all year round. In Connecticut, June is a period of maximum body size and maximum spawning effort and is a reflection of the burst of early summer growth of hydroids on rocks, wharves, and new eelgrass blades.

Tubularia hydroids, because of their pink colour, are easy to spot and may be large and solitary or may be colonial and form pink patches or bushy pompoms. The nudibranchs are not so easy to spot, because they hide among the tangled stolons and stems and lay their eggs at the base of the colonies. The slugs also feed there, piercing a hole in the hydroid's outer plastic-like sheath (perisarc) and then sucking out the soft body tissues (coenosarc).

DISTRIBUTION

Common in Europe from Norway to the Mediterranean, and from eastern Canadian Arctic to New Jersey, from the intertidal to 30 m. In Atlantic Canada recorded only from Halifax, Lunenburg, and Kings counties of Nova Scotia.

COMMENTS

As you would expect, *Cuthona gymnota* has, at the tips of its cerata, cnidosacs loaded with stinging cells stolen from its prey. This is nothing new, but in this species there is a new complication introduced and with it another physiological mystery to fathom.

Whereas most nudibranchs obtain their stinging organelles (nematocysts) from the tentacles of hydroids, corals, or jellyfish, *C. gymnota* feeds at the base of stalks and along stolons, which are structures lacking mature functional stinging cells. One logical explanation is that within the tissues that *C. gymnota* sucks up there may be cells containing young undeveloped nematocysts, and that somehow the slug is capable of storing and nurturing these structures through to the complex, fully differentiated stinging apparatus. Such an accomplishment is about the equivalent of humans eating dried bean seeds with their protochlorophyll and developing photosynthetic green patches in their skin by next weekend.

Cuthona concinna

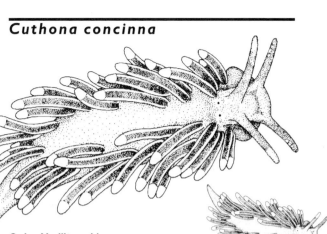

Order: **Nudibranchia**
Suborder: Aeolidacea
Family: Cuthonidae (=Tergipedidae)
Genus: *Cuthona*
Species: *concinna*
Authority: (Alder & Hancock, 1843)

DESCRIPTION

To 15 mm, but usually 5 to 20 mm. A pale, sometimes yellowish slug with diagonal rows of finger-like
cerata, which have white pigment over the tips. Both
the oral and rhinophore tentacles are white tipped
and may have a stripe of white flecks as well. The
digestive gland core of each ceras may be reddish or
brownish but often has an additional violet hue.
Foot is broad with tail short and wide.

NATURAL HISTORY

This inconspicuous species of *Cuthona* is typically
found on large bushy hydroid colonies of the genera
Halecium, *Sertularia*, and *Tubularia*. These large
hydroids grow well in strong currents. Two interesting sites where they usually host *Cuthona concinna* are
the rushing tidal waters of both the Bear River and

Annapolis River, where these empty into the Annapolis Basin of Nova Scotia.

Very little has been written concerning this species. The scattered reports from Atlantic Canada include the months January, March, July, September, October, and November, but nothing is known of spawning seasons or of how many generation per year.

DISTRIBUTION

From Norway to the Normandy coast of France, from Nova Scotia to New Jersey, and from Alaska to southern British Columbia. Recorded in Atlantic Canada from both sides of Bay of Fundy, and from Atlantic coast of Nova Scotia.

COMMENTS

Studying the genus *Cuthona* could turn you into a "mad scientist"—"mad" in both senses of the word: you could get very angry and you could be driven insane. *Cuthona* has had, at various times and places, the following aliases: *Eolis, Cratenopsis, Cavolina, Njurja, Narraeolidia, Toorna, Selva, Xenocratena, Catriona, Precuthona,* and *Trinchesia.* Only recently, with more and better equipped nudibranch researchers, has it been established that all those genera are one and the same. Now, wouldn't that make you mad if you had spent years trying to learn how to tell all those genera apart?

It is now known that *Cuthona* is a circumpolar genus with many similar species, which themselves may have several colour varieties. Over the past 150 years naturalists in many European countries, on the east and west coasts of North America, and in Japan have merrily bestowed scientific names upon their local species not realizing that their "discovery" had already been "discovered" several times and places previously. They even created all those new genera in a desperate attempt to help organize all those new species into smaller groups. Even today there are about two dozen "good" species of *Cuthona* in Europe and another 60 species around the world, with new species being discovered rather regularly (1977, '78, '79, '80, '81, '85, '86, '87) on the West Coast of North America. We may well have several undescribed species in Atlantic Canada, for I have seen a few specimens that didn't quite fit in where I wanted them to. It can drive you crazy trying to decide whether to make a specimen fit in or to make it into a new species!

How fascinating that such tiny creatures, hidden away in the ocean's depths, have been able to persuade research scientists to change their minds so many times. Aren't you thankful that you didn't become a nudibranch specialist until the 1990s?

Cuthona pustulata

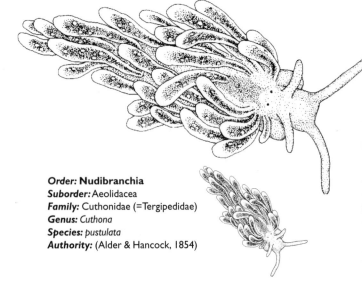

Order: **Nudibranchia**
Suborder: Aeolidacea
Family: Cuthonidae (=Tergipedidae)
Genus: *Cuthona*
Species: *pustulata*
Authority: (Alder & Hancock, 1854)

DESCRIPTION

To 18 mm. Body slender, translucent white, with
long tail and yellowish or reddish-brown cerata.
Most distinctive feature is scattered patches of white
pigment on cerata and tentacles and the lack of any
other colour patterns. Even the tips of the cerata are
clear, and the typical *Cuthona* finger-like shape is
often distorted into club-shaped or swollen-tipped
cerata, hence the species name *pustulata*.

NATURAL HISTORY

This is a species of deeper waters, recorded from
depths of 10 to 33 m, feeding on hydroids of the genus *Halecium*. In Europe, *C. pustulata* spawns from
May to August, and there is indirect evidence for direct development. In North America, however, data
from 1977 to 1982 in British Columbia demonstrated

a May spawning, a hatching of planktotrophic veliger larvae, and a disappearance of all adults in June. The West Coast habitat was in an area of strong currents between islands, as was the Nova Scotia locality, a narrows of rip currents between East Ferry and Long Island, Digby County.

The three small (8-mm) specimens of *Cuthona pustulata* found at East Ferry on 14 October 1970 constitute the first (and probably only) geographic record of this species from the considerable distributional gap between British Columbia and England. Thus we now know it occurs in the western Atlantic, but our knowledge of its natural history in the Atlantic Canada region could be inscribed upon the head of a pin.

DISTRIBUTION

France, British Isles, Denmark, Iceland, southwest Nova Scotia, and extreme southern British Columbia.

COMMENTS

If you thoughtfully consider the geographic history of this species, your thoughts should lead to a revealing conclusion. (See below if your thoughts are not in a leading mood today.)

From 1854 until 1984, *Cuthona pustulata* was strictly a "European" species. From 1977 to 1982, Millen collected the first specimens from the Pacific Ocean region near Saltspring and Galiano islands in southern British Columbia and reported her studies in 1984. The three 1970 specimens from near Digby, Nova Scotia, were not correctly identified until 1989. These specimens were a lucky find, because *C. pustulata* is a subtidal scuba species and was found intertidally in the Bay of Fundy only because our Atlantic Canada highest/lowest tides in the world are the equivalent of Moses parting the seas, thus rendering it possible to walk the ocean floor sans scuba.

Revealing conclusion: an intertidal faunal list of sea slugs (which is the basis of this book) is just the tip of the nudibranch iceberg. No one should be surprised if dredge and grab samples and scuba exploration beyond the low-tide zone add several "Mediterranean," "British," "West Coast," or even "Japanese" species to our Atlantic Canada list.

Cuthona nana

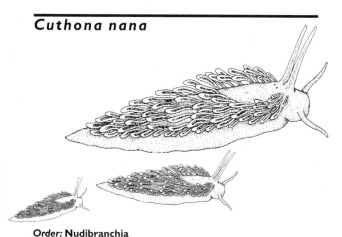

Order: Nudibranchia
Suborder: Aeolidacea
Family: Cuthonidae (=Tergipedidae)
Genus: *Cuthona*
Species: *nana*
Authority: (Alder & Hancock, 1842)

DESCRIPTION

To 28 mm. Body, head, and foot are broad to the extent that much of the dorsum is bare, with the numerous club-shaped cerata limited to the sides. Many of the smaller anterior cerata are even located beside and in front of the rhinophores. Cerata cores are reddish brown, but the overall body colour is pinkish, with a translucent skin in which numerous, minute, white epidermal glands are just discernable. The tentacles are colourless or at most whitish towards the tips.

NATURAL HISTORY

Cuthona nana is an unusual specialist, for it preys only upon the hydroid *Hydractinia echinata*, which in turn grows only upon snail shells, which in turn are occupied only by hermit crabs. The colonial hydroid is as fascinating as the associated stinging nudibranch and spiral-bodied crab, for *Hydractinia* secretes a skeletal framework over the snail shell of a hard but porous crust, festooned with rigid spines. The spines protect the soft hydroid polyps from being scraped and shredded as the hermit crab travels across the ocean floor in his zero-clearance camper.

Cuthona nana's broad foot and body conform to the sheet-like structure of its prey. The slug's pink colour is derived from the pink hydroid and is richest when the nudibranch consumes the female members of *Hydractinia* colonies, for appropriately, and unlike the males, they are clothed in shocking pink.

In Maine and New Hampshire, at depths beyond 5 m, *Cuthona nana* was found throughout the year but was more common in spring and summer, when as many as eight nudibranchs decorated a single hermit crab house. In Nova Scotia *Hydractinia*-coated snail shells are often seen during periods of extreme low tides in the Bay of Fundy, but *C. nana* has yet to be discovered.

DISTRIBUTION

Not yet reported from Atlantic Canada but included here because this species is common in Maine and Europe, and on the Pacific coast where it is currently referred to as *Cuthona divae* (Marcus, 1961), seemingly for historical reasons.

COMMENTS

Actually, the relationships of this unusual trio of empty snail shell, hermit crab, and nudibranch is not as simple as outlined above. In our latitude, if the crab abandons its snail home, the hydroid colony dies. In the Arctic, *Hydractinia* grow on empty snail shells not having a resident hermit crab. However, at a site with tidal currents of up to 8 knots, at Portsmouth, Maine, *Hydractinia* grew on rocks, wooden pilings, and algal holdfasts, forming patches to 30 cm in diameter, and was crawling with *C. nana*. That was a totally unexpected discovery. There are swift tidal currents at many sites in Atlantic Canada, so all encrusting pink hydroid patches should be examined most carefully for this elusive aeolid.

Cuthona viridis

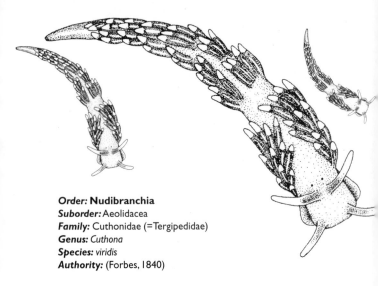

Order: **Nudibranchia**
Suborder: Aeolidacea
Family: Cuthonidae (=Tergipedidae)
Genus: Cuthona
Species: viridis
Authority: (Forbes, 1840)

DESCRIPTION

To 20 mm. Body whitish or pale yellow and semi-translucent, whereas tentacles are opaque white. The cerata are distinctive in being green with scattered flecks of black pigment, and in possessing large white cnidosacs that fill the tip of each ceras. There may be a white line or row of white pigment specks on the anterior face of each ceras.

NATURAL HISTORY

In Europe, *C. viridis* occurs intertidally and subtidally, where it preys upon several genera of hydroids, the stinging cells of which it stores in those large cnidosacs.

DISTRIBUTION

A cool-water species, it is common in northern France, around the British Isles, Iceland, and Greenland. A single 1970 specimen from East Ferry, Digby County, Nova Scotia, is the first official report from North America. However, Thompson and Brown (1984) are of the opinion that *Cuthona albocrusta* of the U.S. west coast, as well as *C. signifera* of Japan and *C. scintillans* of New Zealand, are in fact the one and only green *Cuthona viridis* (which is indicative of how poorly traveled are the slug specialists in each country as compared to the slugs they are studying). If they are correct, then the discovery of this green aeolid in Atlantic Canada was only a matter of time.

COMMENTS

Although collected in 1970, the Digby County specimen was not examined carefully until November 1990, and only then was its true identity determined. To neglect discovering this species for 20 years, dear reader, does deserve a word of explanation.

The little (3-mm) sea slug in question was found in the laboratory while searching through a tray of entangled blue mussels and hydroids: a tray from which eight other species of nudibranchs had already been extracted. The specimen had been injured and was in a contracted state and thus unsuitable for a photographic record. As this slimy blob was green, I assumed it was an algal eater, yet it looked more like a carnivorous aeolid. So it was preserved in alcohol, with a label marked "aeolid?" and set aside for some future rainy day.

In the intervening 20 years, I was kept busy investigating those other species that had been correctly identified. Conveniently, during those two decades, there developed an ever-accelerating increase in sea slug research, seemingly all over the world. The ensuing theses, papers, monographs, and field guides have enhanced the possibilities of valid identifications immeasurably. In museum research, time lags of decades between collection and final identification are not uncommon. You can collect a specimen in five minutes, but it may well take five years to give it a name. This is why proper professional storage facilities (meaning equipment and staff) are fundamental to, and the backbone of, any institution that aspires to qualify as a true museum. As a responsible repository, a museum must assume that the initial storage period of any of its acquisitions will be about 100 years.

Thus, over time, old collections accumulate and then yield new studies and produce new information. By such means does the possibility of identifying some of "ye olde unknownes" inexorably advance. So, when I rediscovered vial "aeolid? 1970" in November 1990, I simply dissected the slug's head, removed the radular ribbon tongue, examined the teeth under a microscope, and consulted the charts of teeth published by Thompson and Brown in 1984. The teeth matched those of *Cuthona viridis,* and my old field notes on morphology and pigment pattern agreed exactly with Thompson and Brown's text. It was that easy, in the 1990s, to discover this first record of *C. viridis* for Nova Scotia and the first specimen from the western Atlantic.

Tenellia fuscata

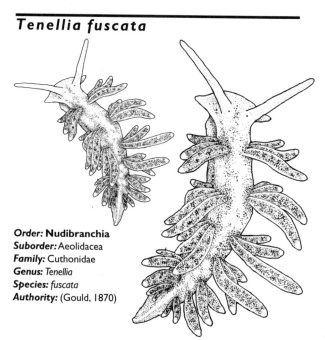

Order: **Nudibranchia**
Suborder: Aeolidacea
Family: Cuthonidae
Genus: *Tenellia*
Species: *fuscata*
Authority: (Gould, 1870)

DESCRIPTION

To 8 mm, but usually 3 to 6 mm. Body an inconspicuous dull yellowish brown, with cerata in distinct
dorsolateral rows, only one pair of long tentacles,
and an oral hood that extends laterally to a short
tentacle.

NATURAL HISTORY

This tiny species (and its European equivalent
T. pallida) is tolerant of high temperatures and low
salinities and thrives in estuarine conditions, even
through the heat of summer. It preys upon a variety
of hydroids, including some solitary species, which it
finds by crawling along algal filaments and the stems
of marine angiosperms such as widgeon grass,
Ruppia maritima. Studies in Connecticut revealed
that when *T. fuscata* finds a hydroid colony it feeds

and then lays as many as 2,700 eggs, in little clusters of 30 to 40, before dying of old age in about 30 days. The eggs develop into slugs in five to nine days and are themselves old enough to start spawning in another 10 days. Such reproductive capabilities can generate densities of 1,100 *T. fuscata* individuals per gram of hydroid colony, which usually results in the total destruction of that particular food source.

One should not be misled by the low salinity and heat-tolerant reputation of this nudibranch, for in Nova Scotia it not only occurs in pools on tidal estuarine marshes but also on hydroids from 15-m depths in Minas Basin, and on subtidal hydroids of rocks and channel buoys from Atlantic waters of coastal Lunenburg County. The few Nova Scotia records are, however, all from summer months, so we do not yet know where *T. fuscata* hangs out from September to June in Atlantic Canada. If this species does die of old age every 30 days, then it must be spawning somewhere locally almost every month of the year.

DISTRIBUTION

This species is limited to the east coast of North America, from Nova Scotia to Virginia. As it occurs on the Atlantic coast of Nova Scotia, it must surely be widespread in the other Maritime provinces.

COMMENTS

As you can imagine, finding this tiny creature is a challenge. You could gather up tons of algae or hydroid-covered mussel shells and spend weeks sorting through it with a hand lens and binocular microscope and find something, or find nothing. Fortunately, in the field, *Tenellia fuscata* advertises its presence because, being such a prolific egg layer, its little, white, jelly-bean egg masses are glued all over the hydroid stems, and that is what you must look for. Scrape off those egg-festooned hydroids, and although you may not notice any slugs at first glance, there probably are dozens there, very effectively mimicking the hydroids.

Tergipes tergipes

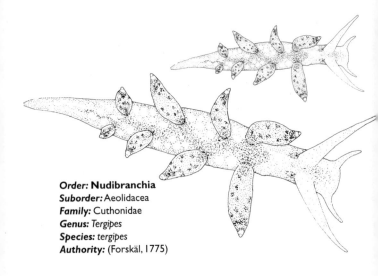

Order: **Nudibranchia**
Suborder: Aeolidacea
Family: Cuthonidae
Genus: *Tergipes*
Species: *tergipes*
Authority: (Forskäl, 1775)

DESCRIPTION

To 8 mm, but more usually 4 to 6 mm. This long,
slender aeolid is easily recognized by the eight (or
even fewer) large, singly placed cerata, each with
a conspicuous white, apical, defensive cnidosac.
Cerata are serially connected at their bases by a
brown, zigzag digestive tract. The bright, cream-
coloured gonads show through the nearly transparent body wall, which has flecks of brown pigment
scattered over it and the cerata, and clustered at
the bases of the tentacles.

NATURAL HISTORY

Tergipes tergipes is one of those opportunistic, short-
lived, carnivorous species forever questing after new
hydroid colonies. It has been found throughout the
year and apparently is capable of producing eggs at

any time. In Connecticut, egg production takes a jump in May and June in response to increased growth and reproduction by hydroids at this time of year, in particular by the ubiquitous species of *Obelia* (= *Laomedea*). These hydroids occur on rocks, pebbles, kelp, eelgrass, mussel shells, floating docks, mooring lines, boat hulls, and navigational buoys: in other words, just about everywhere. Sociable little *T. tergipes* may be found sharing its banquet table with several species of *Eubranchus* or *Doto* or *Dendronotus frondosus* or even *Tenellia fuscata*. Every collection of hydroid colonies should, therefore, be examined most carefully, for with this potential mix of species you have a fine opportunity to add to both your Provincial List and your Life List of "Sea Slugs I Have Encountered."

DISTRIBUTION

Reported in Europe from the Mediterranean Sea to Norway; from Iceland; in North America from Newfoundland to New Jersey; in Sao Paulo, Brazil, in the South Atlantic; and in New Caledonia in the southwest Pacific. In Atlantic Canada, *T. tergipes* is so far recorded from Logy Bay, Newfoundland; St. Andrews, New Brunswick; and many localities in Nova Scotia covering the Minas Basin, Bay of Fundy, and Atlantic coast.

COMMENTS

A geographic distribution such as the above, and there are other similar examples, is bothersome to many scientists. It is untidy, and it begs an explanation. Scientists are trained to organize their facts and their thoughts and thereby discover neat patterns that fit into categories. It is bothersome to discover an animal species that is scattered about the globe. Why does *Tergipes tergipes* not have a limited geographic range, as do most species? Seeking an answer to this question has generated some very heated arguments among scientists.

Historically, one of the following two hypotheses has often been proven to be applicable in such situations. The first is that the geographic distribution appears fragmented, because too few persons have tried to find the creature, and with time the apparent gaps will fill in. For example, an undescribed species of *Tergipes* was reported from California in 1980, and it may prove to be the first record of *T. tergipes* from that coast.

The second suggested solution is the neatest, because it argues that the distant populations may in fact be different species, as yet unrecognized because no competent slug specialist has examined them carefully. Unfortunately, in most cases when they finally are examined, they do turn out to be the same species.

A third plausible hypothesis is of an entirely different nature and is very disturbing, because it is almost impossible to prove or disprove, short of DNA-sequencing comparisons. The implications in regard to scholarly zoogeographic and phytogeographic studies are shattering. It suggests that in the days of sail and wooden ships, whole communities of "fouling organisms" attached to ships' hulls were transported throughout the seven seas and transplanted on foreign shores. What fouled the ships' hulls, and created considerable drag, was a coating of bushy hydroids and bryozoans, anemones, barnacles, tube worms, tunicates, and algae.

To combat this buildup, ships were regularly careened, that is, tipped on their sides and scraped clean. What was the fate of all those scrapings of hydroids and sea slugs from British vessels newly arrived in Brazil or Australia? Could such a community have even survived passage across the equator, with changes in temperature and salinity, and even new predators? It is a real possibility. Or is *Tergipes* in southern Brazil, because it was already hanging about coastlines when the Atlantic Ocean was born and simply expanded its range as that new basin gradually expanded?

Cratena pilata

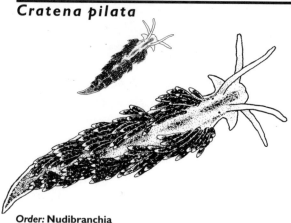

Order: **Nudibranchia**
Suborder: Aeolidacea
Family: Phidianidae (=Facelinidae)
Genus: *Cratena*
Species: *pilata*
Authority: (Gould, 1870)

DESCRIPTION

To 30 mm. Body similar in shape to coryphellids,
with long tentacles and laterally extended, hooked,
anterior foot margins. Colour pattern differs from
coryphellids in being greyish to greenish grey with
white margin around the body, white-tipped cerata,
and much white on the tentacles. The most distinctive colour character is the middorsal row of rusty
brown patches. The dark digestive gland lobe
within each ceras is peculiarly knotted and knobby.

NATURAL HISTORY

This species is unusual in its ability to thrive in
estuarine conditions of low salinity. Most reports
are from bays and harbours where it obviously preys
upon stinging hydroids and jellyfish, for its cerata

are loaded with nematocysts, as many as 50 to 800 in the cnidosac of each ceras. The larger jellyfish of our inshore waters have a sessile life history stage of tiny, colonial, hydroid-like polyps, which are attached to rocks, shells, and wharf pilings. *Cratena pilata* specializes in consuming this attached form of jellyfish, which nevertheless already has the stinging capabilities of the drifting adults. The nudibranch slug consumes the intended defensive nematocysts with impunity and sequesters these undischarged weapons at the tips of its cerata.

DISTRIBUTION

Reported from North Carolina to Massachusetts Bay, but not from the upper Bay of Fundy as yet. It is an endemic western Atlantic species, first discovered in the estuary of the Charles River at Boston by A. A. Gould in the 1860s. Tidal rivers are usually bypassed by nudibranch hunters in preference for the clean, salty seacoast, but in the case of this species, rotting boat hulls, old ballast rocks, and derelict wharf pilings should be examined on low tides— if you can find a non-toxic river estuary.

COMMENTS

Cratena pilata has a special claim to fame because it was this species that Kepner studied in his classic 1943 investigation of nematocysts. He was the first scientist to attempt to follow the actual transfer of intact nematocyst bodies (organelles) from the skin of the cnidarian prey to the skin of the aeolid nudibranch predator. Please note that Kepner's observations, which constituted a major advance, took place 100 years after the microscopists of the 1840s discovered "thread bodies" in sea slugs. Why such a long time? The reasons are sad but instructive and should be told. In essence, not all scientists are exemplary, suitable role models. There are those more interested in advancement of self than advancement of their subject. Their own pet theories must remain correct in spite of evidence to the contrary, and to provide sustaining proof becomes an obsession. Predictably, this perverse pursuit eventually ends with the self-destruction of what once was an esteemed reputation. The powers of incisive, objective thinking become inversely proportional to an ever-expanding ego.

To naturalists of the 1840s, the nematocysts released from the tips of nudibranch cerata certainly resembled sperm and therefore were declared such by the "establishment" scientists. However, in 1858 an independent investigator in Scotland, T. Strethill Wright, pointed out that there was not an anatomical connection with reproductive organs and, more importantly, that the "sperm" varied in morphology, a morphology always identical with that of the nematocysts of whatever species of cnidarian the sea slug had just consumed. Wright's subsequent publication of 1859 was ignored, as was his further report of 1861. Not until 1903 did anyone prove beyond a reasonable doubt that Wright was right.

The "Great Ones" in science had soon conceded that, yes, those structures were "stinging bodies" and not sperm, but, they argued, because true nematocysts were defensive organelles, then they must defend an organism and could not reasonably be transferred intact, fully loaded, and undischarged to the skin of a predator to serve the very same function. End of scientific debate. As these leading scientists (including sea slug expert R. Bergh) could not imagine such a transfer happening, they then had to propose an alternative hypothesis, and prove it. Easy. The slugs must generate their own stinging cells from cells lining the cnidosac, and it was just coincidental that they closely resemble the nematocysts of jellyfish and hydrozoans. So, from the late 1850s into 1902, various investigators published their research "discoveries" and actually described all the developmental stages necessary to prove their hypothesis. Finally, in 1903, Grosvenor rediscovered Wright's research reports, repeated the experiments, and added a few of his own and ended nearly a half century of shameful science.

Forty years later (1943), Kepner at the University of Virginia, actually traced the transfer of nematocysts over minutes and hours. He discovered that *Cratena pilata*, when fed the hydrozoan *Permaria tiarella* and its six types of nematocysts, digests the cells (cnidoblasts) that contain the nematocysts in its stomach chamber and then (somehow) selectively moves these released organelles into the digestive gland lobes of the cerata. Although food particles are taken up and consumed by digestive cells in the cerata, the nematocysts are spared, and they all continue through a canal into the cnidosac where all are engulfed by the cells lining this chamber. It is here that five of the six nematocyst types are digested, while the very useful sixth type is steadily accumulated. How do the cnidosac cells decide which nematocyst types are to be digested and which not?

In 1982, Cargo and Burnett investigated the tissues of *Cratena pilata* with modern microscopical techniques, including the electron microscope. They determined that a 12-mm *C. pilata* may have 45 cerata, and each ceras may have accumulated 500 to 1,000 nematocysts, which it releases, when irritated, in batches of 25 to 50 at a time.

Consider the time lapses between 1858, 1903, 1943, and 1982 and accept that the wheels of discovery oftimes turn unduly slowly. A few clues have accumulated, but several fundamental questions are yet to be answered. How do cnidosac cells select only the most effective nematocysts, and not always the same ones, from whatever mixture they are offered? Why consume and digest unwanted nematocysts instead of rejecting them outright and ejecting them via the cnidosac pore? Could the slugs be distributing toxins from digested nematocysts to their own cells?

Facelina bostoniensis

Order: **Nudibranchia**
Suborder: Aeolidacea
Family: Phidianidae
Genus: *Facelina*
Species: *bostoniensis*
Authority: (Couthouy, 1838)

DESCRIPTION

To 55 mm in Europe, but usually 5 to 30 mm in North America. Overall appearance of this nudibranch is distinctive: a very broad foot, a wide body that is broadest at the "shoulders," and two very long, curved oral tentacles held forward in a manner reminiscent of the long-horned steers of cowboy lore.

In the head region, internal organs impart a rosy hue. Cerata are basic beige but can vary towards reddish or greyish. They have a few white pigment blotches scattered along their forward edge, with the largest white patch at a subapical position. Leading edge of the broad foot has tentaculiform corners, and the distinctive rhinophores are decorated with 20 to 30 encircling lamellae, reminiscent of a Japanese pagoda.

This species has yet another aesthetic attribute: its white egg string is carefully cemented to the sea floor in a lovely expanding pattern of successive and concentric loops. No other nudibranch takes this much trouble to decorate its surroundings.

NATURAL HISTORY

Very little is known about this species in North America, but in Europe its hydroid prey includes *Obelia*, *Clava*, *Bougainvillia*, *Eudendrium*, *Sertularia*, *Dynamena*, and *Tubularia*. Near Belfast, Ireland, *F. bostoniensis* was found from March to late October in empty sandstone burrows of rock-boring clams. In Atlantic Canada, the same or related species of clams create the same mini-habitat in our soft-rock shorelines, but as yet we have no reports of *F. bostoniensis* from such cavities.

Long-term studies in Denmark revealed that there are two generations per year, with the first spawning period in May and June corresponding with the sea-sonal increase in hydroid prey. The June-spawning *F. bostoniensis* are 9 to 10 months of age and die im-mediately after. In late September and October the new generation, only three to four months old, spawns, and this time the stimulus is a profusion of scyphistoma polyps, which are the tiny, sessile, overwintering hydroid stage of the large jellyfish we see in the summer months. Even at this proto-jellyfish stage, there are tentacles equipped with nasty stinging cells, but *F. bostoniensis* was observed to immobilize the polyps with a coating of thick mucus and then consume the entire animal in one bite. Remember that many of those stinging cells are not digested, but are transferred intact to a sac at the tip of each ceras and become part of the *bostoniensis* deterrent.

DISTRIBUTION

Norway to western Mediterranean Sea and Nova
Scotia to Connecticut. Records are sparse in North
America, and in Atlantic Canada all specimens thus
far have come from either Minas Basin or Annapolis
Basin, Nova Scotia.

COMMENTS

Have you been wondering why a European sea slug
has a name honouring Boston, Massachusetts? It is
an interesting story and reveals what goes on behind
the scenes of the printed page. It has to do with the
Rule of Priority, one of a host of rules established by
learned members of the International Commission
on Zoological Nomenclature (ICZN), the highest
court in the biological realm. The commissioners
are the top guns who maintain law and order within a
subculture of eccentric, overzealous taxonomists
who collect and put names to creatures and publish,
publish, publish. Over the past two centuries, different biologists in different geographic regions at
different times have often placed the name of their
choice upon the very same animal. The Rule of
Priority simply states that the lucky person who first
found, described, and named a creature wins.
Everyone else must swallow their pride and relegate
their carefully considered name to the wastebasket.
Interestingly, the ICZN keeps track of what is in
the wastebasket and has a special set of rules that
determine which names on the discard list can or
cannot be recycled.

  References to sea slugs in the European literature
go back to the year 1554, so, as you might expect,
most sea slugs with an amphiatlantic distribution

were discovered and named by Europeans long before North American naturalists got up steam. However, the Europeans did miss one, and specimens from the harbour at Boston, Massachusetts, were the first to receive scientific attention. In 1838 they were properly described by Joseph Pitty Couthouy in the *Boston Journal of Natural History*.

Then the British discovered it and named it *curta* in 1843. The Irish named it *drummondi* in 1844. The Norwegians introduced *auriculata* in 1939, and the confusion continued until 1981, when finally a Britisher sorted it all out and admitted that the name provided by an obscure naturalist from the colonies actually did have priority. It is somewhat ironic for the British that one of their native nudibranchs should bear the name of the site of the Boston Tea Party, a celebration that precipitated events leading to the loss of half of British North America to an independent United States of America.

Aeolidia papillosa

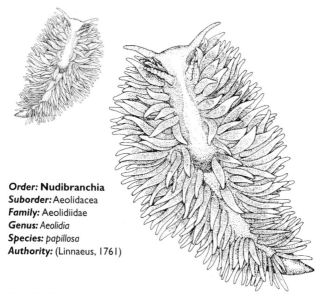

Order: Nudibranchia
Suborder: Aeolidacea
Family: Aeolidiidae
Genus: Aeolidia
Species: papillosa
Authority: (Linnaeus, 1761)

DESCRIPTION

Our largest nudibranch, reaching 120 mm in the record book, but local specimens are half that size. Overall appearance is of a pale to dark brown, mottled, stocky, very furry sea slug. Numerous cerata practically obscure the body, and when *Aeolidia papillosa* is disturbed it contracts its body and looks much like a prickly hedgehog. Cerata have distinct white tips and differ from the norm in being flattened and overlapping, accounting for the visual effect of body fur.

NATURAL HISTORY

In the Bay of Fundy most spawning activity takes place from February to June. The young grow rapidly, but in spite of their large size rarely live beyond two years. *Aeolidia papillosa* does not rely upon various ephemeral hydroid colonies as an energy source.

It is a specialist, and its prey is the giant sea anemone *Metridium senile*, which is so tough and so defended by chemicals and stinging cells that *A. papillosa* essentially has this abundant, year-round food supply all to itself. Nevertheless, there are risks accompanying this fat-cat lifestyle. Crawling about on exposed rock surfaces and over the bare surface of the anemones, this nudibranch is exposed to those fish predators that hunt visually. The slug attempts to minimize this danger by loading its cerata with anemone nematocysts, by being nocturnal, and by resting in a contracted position so that it and its cerata resemble an anemone with tentacles expanded. Note that these false tentacles can actually deliver true nematocyst stings. However, in spite of these precautions there is one relentless fish, the common sea perch or cunner, *Tautogolabrus adspersus*, that actively hunts for and swallows small (not large) nudibranchs, including *A. papillosa*.

A second risk entails getting too close to a large *Metridium senile*, for if really annoyed this anemone may unleash its killer threads. These are long, thin, nematocyst-laden threads, which can quietly slide out of hidden pores in the body wall. If one of these threads becomes entangled in the slug's cerata, the subsequent massive injection of nematocyst toxins can kill the nudibranch. To summarize: once a *Metridium senile* gets big enough it is safe from nudibranch attacks, and once *Aeolidia papillosa* becomes large enough it is safe from fish attacks. It is those months in between that are rough.

DISTRIBUTION

This circumpolar anemone predator occurs throughout boreal and subarctic seas as far south as France, Maryland, California, and Japan. It ranges vertically from tidal pools to depths of 800 m.

COMMENTS

When seized by a predator, the almost universal response of a vertebrate is a scream, which serves chiefly to warn others of the immediate danger. The terror scream of a frog and a rabbit and a human are remarkably alike. Plants and many invertebrates cannot produce a vocal scream, but they accomplish the same ends by means of chemical screams. Such compounds, termed pheromones, are released by the victim and are wafted away by air currents or water currents. When the molecules are absorbed by neighbouring individuals, they elicit defensive behavioural responses. Even trees, when attacked by hordes of caterpillars, can inform and alarm other trees through such airborne chemical messages. Pheromones are a sort of aerosol hormone and are extensively employed by invertebrates for organizing family affairs, love affairs, and warfares.

When an anemone is attacked by *A. papillosa*, it not only fights back with its killer threads but as well generates a panic pheromone that alerts and alarms nearby anemones. They respond by contracting and withdrawing their tender oral discs and tentacles, as these are the favourite attack sites of *A. papillosa*. As it dies, the unfortunate anemone victim contributes to a marvelous revengeful twist. As the nudibranch consumes the anemone, it also consumes the alarm pheromone, which then emanates from the slug for as long as five days. So, although that *Aeolidia papillosa* did find a patch of expanded anemones and got one meal, for the rest of the week the poor slug becomes a walking security alarm, screaming chemically at every anemone that it so carefully tries to approach.

Conclusions

In this century we humans have learned that survival on this planet requires a comprehensive understanding of nature, from the ozone layer to the abyssal ooze. We have also discovered that biochemically all living creatures are mitochondrial brothers and sisters under one sun. We have also begun to realize that natural phenomena seem infinitely complex and individual organisms infinitely variable. Therefore, every clue, every unlocked secret, advances our hopes of ever understanding that truly awesome system we term Planet Earth.

If you have read the comments paragraphs in the species descriptions section of this little book, you should now realize that even the lowly sea slug can assist us in our perpetual quest toward a better understanding of ourselves and our world. One of the enticing excitements of scientific investigation is that your research results may be just what you hoped for, may not be worth the paper upon which they are written, or may change the minds of humankind forever after. For most scientists the intellectual thrills are worth the long tedious hours and the numerous methodological frustrations.

We who work with nudibranchs and sacoglossans have an advantage denied the rest of the research fraternity. When suffering from the fatigue of frustration, we simply contemplate our research organisms from an aesthetic point of view, and such beauty, yea fit for a queen, is restorative beyond measure.

References

REFERENCES FOR PARTICULAR SPECIES

Limacina retroversa, helicina

Lalli, Carol M., and Fred E. Wells. 1978. Reproduction in the genus *Limacina* (Opisthobranchia: Thecosomata). *J. Zool. Lond.* 186: 95–108.

Lalli, Carol M., and Ronald W. Gilmer. 1989. *Pelagic snails: The biology of holoplanktonic gastropod mollusks.* Stanford, Calif.: Stanford University Press.

Newman, Leslie J. 1981. The distribution and biology of pteropods from the Bay of Fundy region, Canada (Gastropods: Opisthobranchia). M.Sc. thesis, Dept. Zool., Univ. Guelph, Ontario.

Clione limacina

Lalli, Carol. 1970. Structure and function of the buccal apparatus of *Clione limacina* (Phipps) with a review of feeding in gymnosomatous pteropods. *J. Exp. Mar. Biol. Ecol.* 4: 101–18.

Alderia modesta

Bleakney, J. Sherman. 1988. The radula and penial style of *Alderia modesta* (Lovén, 1844) (Opisthobranchia: Ascoglossa) from populations in North America and Europe. *Veliger* 31(3/4): 226–35.

Bleakney, J. S., and K. B. Meyer. 1979. Observations on salt-marsh pools, Minas Basin, Nova Scotia. *Proc. Nova Scotia Inst. Sci.* 29: 353–71.

Evans, T. J. 1953. The alimentary and vascular systems of *Alderia modesta* (Lovén) in relation to its ecology. *Proc. Malacol. Soc. London* 29(6): 249–58.

Graves, Debra A., M. A. Gibson, and J. S. Bleakney. 1979. The digestive diverticula of *Alderia modesta* and *Elysia chlorotica* (Opisthobranchia: Sacoglossa) *Veliger* 21(4): 415–22.

Hand, C., and J. Steinberg. 1955. On the occurrence of the nudibranch *Alderia modesta* (Lovén, 1844) on the central California coast. *Nautilus* 69(1): 22–28.

Trowbridge, Cynthia D. 1993. Local and regional abundance patterns of the Ascoglossan (= Sacoglossan) opisthobranch *Alderia modesta* (Lovén, 1844) in the northeastern Pacific. *Veliger* 36 (4): 303–10.

Placida dendritica

Bleakney, J. Sherman. 1989. Morphological variation in the radula of *Placida dendritica* (Alder and Hancock, 1843) (Opisthobranchia: Ascoglossa/Sacoglossa) from Atlantic and Pacific populations. *Veliger* 32(2): 171–81.

Bleakney, J. Sherman. 1990. Indirect evidence of a morphological response in the radula of *Placida dendritica* (Alder and Hancock, 1843) (Opisthobranchia: Ascoglossa/Sacoglossa) to different algal prey. *Veliger* 33(1): 111–5.

Clark, K. B., and D. R. Franz. 1969. Occurrence of the sacoglossan opisthobranch *Hermaea dendritica* Alder and Hancock in New England. *Veliger* 12(2): 174–5.

Thompson, T. E. 1973. Sacoglossan gastropod molluscs from eastern Australia. *Proc. Malacol. Soc. London* 40(4): 239–51.

Stiliger fuscatus

Bleakney, J. S., and Kaniaulono B. Meyer. 1979. Observations on saltmarsh pools, Minas Basin, Nova Scotia 1965–1977. *Proc. N.S. Inst. Sci.* 29: 353–71.

Gascoigne, T. 1978. The internal anatomy of *Stiliger fuscatus* (Gould, 1870). *Zool. J. Linn. Soc. London* 63: 265–74.

Elysia chlorotica

Dawe, Robert D., and Jeffrey L. C. Wright. 1986. The major polyproprionate metabolites from the sacoglossan mollusc *Elysia chlorotica*. *Tetrahedron Letters* 27(23): 2559–62.

Gibson, Glenys D., Daniel P. Toews, and J. Sherman Bleakney. 1986. Oxygen production and consumption in the Sacoglossan (= Ascoglossan) *Elysia chlorotica* Gould. *Veliger* 28(4): 397–400.

Paul, Valerie J., and Kathryn L. Van Alstyne. 1988. Use of ingested algal diterpenoids by *Elysia halimedae* Macnae (Opisthobranchia: Ascoglossa) as antipredator defenses. *J. Exp. Mar. Biol. Ecol.* 119: 15–29.

Raymond, Bruce G., and J. Sherman Bleakney. 1987. The radula and ascus of *Elysia chlorotica* Gould (Opisthobranchia: Ascoglossa). *Veliger* 29(3): 245–250.

West, Hillary H., June F. Harrigan, and Sidney K. Pierce. 1984. Hybridization of two populations of a marine opisthobranch (*Elysia chlorotica*) with different developmental patterns. *Veliger* 26(3): 199–206.

Elysia catula

Clark, Kerry B., and M. Busacca. 1978. Feeding specificity and chloroplast retention in four tropical ascoglossa with a discussion of the extent of chloroplast symbiosis and the evolution of the Order. *J. Moll. Stud.* 44: 272–282

Clark, Kerry B. 1975. Nudibranch life cycles in the northwest Atlantic and their relationship to the ecology of fouling communities. Helgölander wiss, *Meeresunters* 27: 28–69.

Jensen, Kathe R. 1983. Further notes on the ecology and systematics of *Elysia serca* Marcus (Opisthobranchia, Ascoglossa). *J. Moll. Stud. Suppt.* 12A: 69–72.

Rasmussen, Erik. 1973. The eelgrass vegetation and its communities (and history). *In* Systematics and ecology of the Isefjord marine fauna. *Ophelia* 11: 401–430.

Ancula Gibbosa
In some of the General and regional references.

Okenia ascidicola

Morse, M. Patricia. 1972. Biology of *Okenia ascidicola* spec. nov. (Gastropoda : Nudibranchia). *Veliger* 15(2) : 97–101.

Gosner, Kenneth. 1979. *A field guide to the Atlantic seashore.* Petersen Field Guide Series. Boston : Houghton Mifflin Co. 329 pp. (For information on tunicates.)

Acanthodoris pilosa
General and regional references.

Acanthodoris subquadrata

Alder, J., and A. Hancock. 1845–55. *A monograph of the British nudibranchiate mollusca.* London, Ray Society, Parts 1–7: 438 pp.

Thompson, T. E., and G. H. Brown. 1984. *Biology of the opisthobranch molluscs.* Vol. II. The Ray Society, London. 299 pp.

Adalaria proxima

Havenhand, J. N., and C. D. Todd. 1988. Physiological ecology of *Adalaria proxima* (Alder and Hancock) and *Onchidoris muricata* (Muller) (Gastropoda: Nudibranchia). I. Feeding, growth and respiration. *J. Exp. Mar. Biol. Ecol.* 118(2): 151–72.

Havenhand, J. N., and C. D. Todd. 1988. II. Reproduction. *J. Exp. Mar. Biol. Ecol.* 118(2): 173–89.

Havenhand, J. N., and C. D. Todd. 1988. III. Energy budgets. *J. Exp. Mar. Biol. Ecol.* 118(2): 191–205.

Havenhand, J. N., J. P. Thorpe, and C. D. Todd. 1986. Estimates of biochemical genetic diversity within and between the nudibranch molluscs *Adalaria proxima* (Alder and Hancock) and *Onchidoris muricata* (Muller) (Doridacea: Onchidorididae) *J. Exp. Mar. Biol. Ecol.* 95: 105–11.

Millen, Sandra. 1987. The nudibranch genus *Adalaria*, with a description of a new species from the northeastern Pacific. *Canadian J. Zool.* 65(11): 2696–2702.

Todd, C. D., and J. N. Havenhand. 1985. Preliminary observations on the embryonic and larval development of three dorid nudibranchs (*Adalaria proxima*, *Onchidoris muricata*, and *Archidoris pseudoargus*) *J. Moll. Stud.* 51: 97–99.

Todd, C. D., and J. N. Havenhand. 1989. Nudibranch-bryozoan associations: the quantification of ingestion and some observations on partial predation among Doridoidea. *J. Moll. Stud.* 55: 245–259.

Onchidoris muricata

Harvell, C. Drew. 1984. Predator-induced defense in a marine bryozoan. *Science* 224: 1357–9.

Millen, Sandra V. 1985. The nudibranch genera *Onchidoris* and *Diaphodoris* (Mollusca, Opisthobranchia) in the Northeastern Pacific. *Veliger* 28(1): 80–93.

Todd, C. D. 1978. Gonad development of *Onchidoris muricata* (Müller) in relation to size, age and spawning (Gastropoda: Opisthobranchia). *J. Moll. Stud.* 44: 190–9.

Todd, Christopher D. 1978. Changes in spatial pattern of an intertidal population of the nudibranch mollusc *Onchidoris muricata* in relation to life cycle, mortality, and environmental hetero-geneity. *J. Animal Ecol.* 47: 189–203.

Also: General and regional references and several under *Adalaria proxima*.

Onchidoris bilamellata

Barnes, H., and H. T. Powell. 1954. *Onchidoris fusca* (Müller); a predator of barnacles. *J. Animal Ecol.* 23: 361–363.

Bleakney, J. Sherman, and Constance L. Saunders. 1978. Life history observations on the nudibranch mollusc *Onchidoris bilamellata* in the intertidal zone of Nova Scotia. *Canadian Field-Nat.* 92(1): 82–85

Crampton, D. M. 1977. Functional anatomy of the buccal apparatus of *Onchidoris bilamellata* (Mollusca: Opisthobranchia). *Trans. Zool. Soc. Lond.* 34: 45–86.

Edmunds, Malcolm. 1968. Acid secretion in some species of Doridacea (Mollusca, Nudibranchia). *Proc. Malac. Soc. Lond.* 38: 121–33.

Todd, Christopher D. 1979. The population ecology of *Onchidoris bilamellata* (L.) (Gastropoda: Nudibranchia). *J. Exp. Mar. Biol. Ecol.* 41: 213–255.

Todd, Christopher D. 1981. Ecology of nudibranch molluscs. *Oceanography and Marine Biology, Annual Review.* 19: 141–234.

Issena pacifica

Just, Hanne, and Malcolm Edmunds. 1985. *North Atlantic nudibranchs (mollusca) seen by Henning Lemche.* Ophelia Publ., Marine Biol. Lab., Helsingor, Denmark (p. 60–61).

Lawrence, Pauline, K. W. Strong, P. Pocklington, P. Stewart, and G. B. J. Fader. 1989. *A photographic atlas of the eastern Canadian continental shelf: Scotian Shelf and Grand Banks of Newfoundland.* Maritime Testing (1985) Ltd., 116–900 Windmill Road, Dartmouth, Nova Scotia, B3B 1P7. (Available from G. Fader, Atlantic

Geoscience Centre, Geological Survey of Canada,
Bedford Institute of Oceanography, P. O. Box 1006,
Dartmouth, Nova Scotia, B2Y 4A2.

Palio dubia
General and regional references and field guides.

Palio nothus

Behrens, David W. 1980. *Pacific Coast
Nudibranchs,* Sea Challengers, Los Osos, Calif. 112 pp.

Meyer, K. B. 1971. Distribution and
zoogeography of fourteen species of nudibranchs of
northern New England and Nova Scotia. *Veliger*
14(2): 137–52.

Thompson, T. E., and G. H. Brown. 1984.
Biology of Opisthobranch Molluscs. Vol. II. The Ray
Society, London. 229 pp.

Behrens, David W. 1980. *Pacific Coast Nudibranchs,*
Sea Challengers, Los Osos, Calif. 112 pp.

Meyer, K. B. 1971. Distribution and
zoogeography of fourteen species of nudibranchs of
northern New England and Nova Scotia. *Veliger*
14(2): 137–52.

Thompson, T. E., and G. H. Brown. 1984.
Biology of Opisthobranch Molluscs. Vol. II.
The Ray Society, London. 229 pp.

Cadlina laevis

Barbour, M. A. 1979. A note on the distribution and food preferences of *Cadlina laevis. Nautilus*
93: 61–62.

Gibson, Glenys D., and Fu-Shiang Chia. 1991. Contrasting reproductive modes in two sympatric species of Haminaea (Opisthobranchia: Cephalaspidea). *J. Moll. Stud.* 57 (4), Supplement, T. E. Thompson Memorial Issue: 49–60.

Thompson, T. E. 1967. Direct development in a nudibranch, *Cadlina laevis*, with a discussion of developmental processes in Opisthobranchia. *J. Mar. Biol. Ass.* U. K. 47: 1–22.

Cadlina marginata

Just, Hanne, and Malcolm Edmunds. 1985. North Atlantic nudibranchs (Mollusca) seen by Henning Lemche. *Ophelia,* Suppl. 2, pp. 1–170.

Thompson, Janice E., Roger P. Walker, Stephen J. Wratten, and D. John Faulkner. 1982. A chemical defense mechanism for the nudibranch *Cadlina luteomarginata. Tetrahedron* 38(13): 1865–73.

Dendronotus frondosus

Robilliard, Gordon A. 1970. The systematics and some aspects of the ecology of the genus *Dendronotus* (Gastropoda: Nudibranchia). *Veliger* 12(4): 433–479.

Robilliard, Gordon A. 1972. A new species of *Dendronotus* from the northeastern Pacific with notes on *Dendronotus nana* and *Dendronotus robustus* (Mollusca: Opisthobranchia). *Can. J. Zool.* 50: 421–432.

Dendronotus dalli
See under Dendronotus frondosus.

Just, Hanne, and Malcolm Edmunds. 1985. *North Atlantic nudibranchs (Mollusca) seen by Henning Lemche.* Ophelia Publications, Marine Laboratory, Helsingor, Denmark. pp. 170.

Lemche, Henning. 1976. New British species of *Doto* Oken, 1815 (Mollusca: Opisthobranchia). *J. Mar. Biol. Ass. U.K.* 56: 691–706.

Morrow, C. C., J. P. Thorpe, and B. E. Picton. 1992. Genetic divergence and cryptic speciation in two morphs of the common subtidal nudibranch *Doto coronata* (Opisthobranchia: Dendronotacea; Dotoidae) from the northern Irish Sea. *Marine Ecology Progress Series* 84: 53-61.

Ortea, J. A. 1979. Recommendation for unifying the descriptions of *Doto* Oken, 1915. *Opisthobranch Newsletter* 11(4–6): 2–4.

Coryphella verrucosa

Kuzirian, Alan M. 1979. Taxonomy and biology of four New England coryphellid nudibranchs (Gastropoda: Opisthobranchia). *J. Moll. Stud.* 45: 239–261.

Meyer, K. B. 1971. Distribution and zoogeography of fourteen species of nudibranchs of northern New England and Nova Scotia. *Veliger* 14(2): 137–52.

Coryphella gracilis

Kuzirian, Alan M. 1979. Taxonomy and biology of four New England coryphellid nudibranchs (Gastropoda: Opisthobranchia). *J. Moll. Stud.* 45: 239–261.

Coryphella pellucida

Kuzirian, Alan M. 1979. Taxonomy and biology of four New England coryphellid nudibranchs (Gastropoda: Opisthobranchia). *J. Moll. Stud.* 45: 239–261.

Coryphella salmonacea

Morse, M. Patricia. 1971. Biology and life history of the nudibranch mollusc *Coryphella stimpsoni* (Verrill, 1879). *Biol. Bull.* 140(1): 84–94. (Don't be fooled by the name *stimpsoni*, the animal under discussion was actually *salmonacea*.)

Coryphella nobilis & sp. nov.

Kuzirian, Alan M. 1977. The rediscovery and biology of *Coryphella nobilis* Verrill, 1880, in New England (Gastropoda: Opisthobranchia). *J. Moll. Stud.* 43: 230–240.

Kuzirian, Alan M. 1979. Taxonomy and biology of four New England coryphellid nudibranchs (Gastropoda: Opisthobranchis). *J. Moll. Stud.* 45: 239–261.

Eubranchus exiguus

Edmunds, Malcolm, and Annetrudi Kress. 1969. On the European species of *Eubranchus* (Mollusca Opisthobranchia). J. Mar. Biol. Ass. U. K. 49: 879–912.

Just, Hanne, and Malcolm Edmunds. 1985. *North Atlantic nudibranchs (Mollusca) seen by Henning Lemche.* Ophelia Publ., Marine Biol. Lab., Helsingor, Denmark. pp. 170.

Eubranchus pallidus

Edmunds, Malcolm, and Annetrudi Kress. 1969.
On the European species of *Eubranchus* (Mollusca
Opisthobranchia). *J. Mar. Biol. Ass.* U. K. 49: 879–912.

Moore, G. M. 1964. Shell-less Opisthobranchia.
In *Keys to marine invertebrates of the Woods Hole region*,
ed. R. I. Smith, pp. 153–64. Boston: Spaulding Co.

Eubranchus tricolor

Just, Hanne, and Malcolm Edmunds. 1985.
*North Atlantic nudibranchs (Mollusca) seen by Henning
Lemche.* Ophelia Publ. Marine Biol. Lab.,
Helsingor, Denmark. pp.170.

Rivest, Brian R., and Larry G. Harris. 1976.
Eubranchus tricolor Forbes in the Western Atlantic.
Nautilus 90 (4): 145–7.

Eubranchus olivaceus

Lambert, Walter J. 1991. Coexistence of
hydroid-eating nudibranchs: Recruitment and
non-equalibrial patterns of occurrence. *J. Moll.
Stud.* 57 (4), Supplement, T. E. Thompson
Memorial Issue: 35–47.

Meyer, Kaniaulono Bailey. 1971. Distribution and zoogeography of fourteen species of
nudibranchs of Northern New England and Nova
Scotia. *Veliger* 14(2): 137–52.

O'Donoghue, Charles Henry. 1924. Notes
on the nudibranchiate Mollusca from the Vancouver
Island region. *Trans. Roy. Soc. Canad. Inst.* 15(33): 1–33.

Cuthona gymnota

Harris, Larry G. 1971. Nudibranch associations as symbioses. In: *Aspects of the Biology of Symbiosis.* Ed. Thomas C. Cheng. University Park Press, Baltimore, MD. pp. 79–90.

Cuthona concinna

Millen, Sandra V. 1985. Northern, primitive Tergipedid nudibranchs, with a description of a new species (of *Cuthona*) from the Canadian Pacific. *Can. J. Zool.* 64: 1356–62.

Williams, G. C., and T. M. Gosliner. 1979. Two new species of nudibranchiate molluscs from the west coast of North America, with a revision of the family *Cuthonidae. Zool. J. Linn. Soc.* 67: 203–223.

Cuthona pustulata

Gosliner, T. M., and Sandra V. Millen. 1984. Records of *Cuthona pustulata* (Alder and Hancock, 1854) from the Canadian Pacific. *Veliger* 26(3): 183–7.

Cuthona nana

Folino, Nadine C. 1993. Feeding and growth of the aeolid nudibranch *Cuthona nana* (Alder and Hancock, 1842). *J. Moll. Stud.* (1993) 59: 15–22.

Harris, Larry G., Loren W. Wright, and Brian R. Rivest. 1975. Observations on the occurrence and biology of the aeolid nudibranch *Cuthona nana* in New England waters. *Veliger* 17(3): 264–268.

Rivest, Brian R. 1978. Development of the eolid nudibranch *Cuthona nana* (Alder and Hancock, 1842) and its relationship with a hydroid and hermit crab (in New Hampshire). *Biol. Bull.* 154(1): 157–75.

Cuthona viridis

Thompson, T. E., and G. H. Brown. 1984. *Biology of opisthobranch molluscs,* Vol. II. The Ray Society: London. 229 pp.

Tenellia fuscata

Harris, Larry G., Mark Powers, and Julia Ryan. 1981. Life history studies of the estuarine nudibranch *Tenellia fuscata* (Gould, 1870). *Veliger* 23(1): 70–74.

Tergipes tergipes

In many of the general references, with considerable information in Clark, 1975.

The California *Tergipes* sp. report is in the field guide by Behrens, 1980.

Cratena pilata

Cargo, David G., and Joseph W. Burnett. 1982. Observations on the ultrastructure and defensive behaviour of the cnidosac of *Cratena pilata. Veliger* 24(4): 325–327.

Grosvenor, G. H. 1903. On the nematocysts of aeolids. *Proc. Royal Society,* London 72: 462–486.

Kepner, William A. 1943. The manipulation of nematocysts of *Pennaria tiarella* by *Aeolis pilata. Journal of Morphology* 73: 297–311.

Wright, T. Strethill. 1859. On the cnidae or thread cells of the Eolidae. *Proc. Roy. Philos. Soc.,* Edinburgh 2 : 38–40.

Facelina bostoniensis

Brown, Gregory H. 1981. The taxonomy of the British species of the genus *Facelina* . Alder and Hancock (Opisthobranchia: Nudibranchia). *J. Moll. Stud.* 47: 334–336.

Fisher, N. 1934. Habitat of *Facelina drummondi* (Alder and Hancock). *J. Conchology* 20(1): 24.

Rassmussen, Erik. 1973. Systematics and ecology of the Isefjord marine fauna (Denmark). *Ophelia* II: 1–495. (pp. 270–271).

Aeolidia papillosa

Harris, Larry G. 1986. Size-selective predation in a sea anemone, nudibranch, and fish food chain. *Veliger* 29(1): 38–47.

Harris, Larry G. 1987. Aeolid nudibranchs as predators and prey. *Amer. Malacol. Bull.* 5(2): 287–292.

Howe, Nathan R., and Larry G. Harris. 1978. Transfer of the sea anemone pheromone, anthopleurine, by the nudibranch *Aeolidia papillosa*. *J. Chem. Ecol.* 4(5): 551–561.

REFERENCES—GENERAL AND REGIONAL

Abbott, R. Tucker. 1974. *American seashells.* New York: Van Nostrand Reinhold Co. 663 pp.

Alder, J., and A. Hancock. 1845–55. *A monograph of the British nudibranchiate Mollusca, with figures of all the species*, parts 1–7. London: The Ray Society. 438 pp.

Clark, Kerry B. 1975. Nudibranch life cycles in the Northern Atlantic and their relationship to the ecology of fouling communities. *Hegloländer wiss. Meeresunters.* 27(1): 28–69.

Edmunds, Malcolm. 1966. Protective mechanisms in the Eolidacea (Mollusca Nudibranchia). *J. Linn. Soc. (Zool.)* 47 (308): 27–71.

Edmunds, M., and A. Kress. 1969. On the European species of *Eubranchus* (Mollusca Opisthobranchia). *J. Mar. Biol. Ass. U.K.* 49: 879–912.

Franz, D.R. 1970. Zoogeography of northwest Atlantic opisthobranch molluscs. *Mar. Biol.* 7(2): 171–80.

Gosliner, Terrence M., and Michael T. Ghiselin. 1987, symposium organizers. Symposium on the ecology and evolution of opisthobranch molluscs. *Amer. Malacol. Bull.* 5(2): 183–306.

Gould, A. A., and W. G. Binney. 1870. *Report on the invertebrates of Massachusetts.* Second ed. Wright and Potter, Boston. 524 pp.

Hadfield, Michael G. 1963. The biology of nudibranch larvae. *Oikos* 14: 85–95.

Jaeger, Edmund C. 1978. *A source book of biological names and terms.* Charles C. Thomas, Springfield, Ill. 360 pp.

Just, Hanne, and Malcolm Edmunds. 1985. *North Atlantic nudibranchs (Mollusca) seen by Henning Lemche.* Ophelia Publ., Marine Biol. Lab., Helsingor, Denmark. (Exquisite water colour paintings, with descriptive text, of 72 species.)

Lalli, Carol M., and Ronald W. Gilmer. 1989. *Pelagic snails: The biology of holoplanktonic gastropos mollusks.* Stanford, Calif.: Stanford University Press.

MacFarland, F. M. 1966. Studies of opisthobranchiate mollusks of the Pacific coast of North America. *Mem. Calif. Acad. Sci.* 6: 1–546.

McDonald, Gary. 1986. *Bibliographia Nudibranchia.* Institute Marine Sciences, Univ. Calif., Santa Cruz, California. 332 pp. (4,160 references).

Meyer, K. B. 1971. Distribution and zoogeography of fourteen species of nudibranchs of northern New England and Nova Scotia. *Veliger* 14(2): 137–52.

Millen, S. 1980. Range extensions, new distribution sites, and notes on the biology of opisthobranchs (Mollusca: Gastropoda) in British Columbia. *Can. J. Zool.* 58: 1207–9.

Novaczek, I., and J. McLachlan. 1988. Investigations of the marine algae of Nova Scotia XVII: Vertical and geographic distribution of marine algae on rocky shores of the Maritime Provinces. *Proc. N. S. Inst. Sci.* 38: 91–143.

Oxford University Press. 1991. *Journal of Molluscan Studies*, T. E. Thompson Memorial Issue, Volume 57, Part 4, November, 1991. pp. 242. (Has 23 articles outlining many unanswered questions. Excellent article on the new topic of transepidermal uptake of dissolved free amino acids in seawater by sacoglossans.)

Pruvot-Fol, A. 1954. *Mollusques Opisthobranches.* Faune de France, Paris. 58: 1–460.

Rasmussen, Erik. 1973. Systematics and ecology of te Isefjord marine fauna (Denmark). *Ophelia* 11: 1–495.

Roginskaya, I. S. 1962. The nudibranchiate mollusks of the White Sea in the region of the Biological station of M.G.U. (in) *Biology of the White Sea.* Moscow U., Belam. Biol. Stant. MGU. Biol. Belogo Maria 1: 88–108.

Russell, Henry D. 1971. *Index Nudibranchia, a catalogue for the literature 1554–1965.* Deleware Museum of Natural History, Greenville. 141 pp. (2,400 references).

Scheuer, Paul J. 1990. Some marine elological phenomena: chemical basis and biomedical potential. *Science* 248: 173–7. (An excellent summary of medical aspects, with 51 references.)

Thompson, T. E. 1976. *Biology of opisthobranch molluscs.* Vol. I. The Ray Society: London. 207 pp.

Thompson, T. E., and G. H. Brown. 1984. *Biology of opisthobranch molluscs,* Vol. II. The Ray Society: London. 229 pp.

Todd, Christopher D. 1981. Ecology of nudibranch molluscs. *Oceanography and Marine Biology, Annual Review.* 19: 141–234.

Turgeon, D. D., A. E. Bogan, E. V. Coan, W. K. Emerson, W. G. Lyons, W. L. Pratt, C. F. E. Roper, A. Scheltema, F. G. Thompson, and J. D. Williams. 1988. *Common and scientific names of aquatic invertebrates from the United States and Canada: Mollusks.* American Fisheries Society Special Publication 16. Bethesda, Maryland. 277 pp.

REFERENCES— SACOGLOSSA (=ASCOGLOSSA)

Bleakney, J. S., and K. B. Meyer. 1979. Observation on saltmarsh pools, Minas Basin Nova Scotia 1965–1977. *Proc. N.S. Inst. Sci.* 29: 353–371.

Clark, K. B., and M. Busacca. 1978. Feeding specificity and chloroplast retention in four tropical ascoglossa with a discussion of the extent of chloroplast symbiosis and the evolution of the order. *J. Moll. Stud.* 44: 272–282.

Clark, K. B., and D. Defreese. 1987. Population ecology of Caribbean ascoglossa (Mollusca: Opisthobranchia); a study of specialized algal herbivores. *Amer. Malacol. Bull.* 5(2): 259–280.

Gascoigne, T. 1985. A provisional classification of families of the order Ascoglossa (Gastropoda: Nudibranchiata). *J. Moll. Stud.* 51(1): 8–22.

Jensen, K. R. 1980. A review of sacoglossan diets, with comparative notes in radular and buccal anatomy. *Malacol. Rev.* 13(1–2): 55–77.

Jensen, K. R. 1983. Preliminary index of species of Ascoglossa. Opisthobranch Newsletter 15(3): 9–15.

Thompson, T. E. 1973. Sacoglossan gastropod molluscs from eastern Australia. *Proc. Malacol. Soc. Lond.* 40 (4): 239–251.

REFERENCES—FIELD GUIDES

Behrens, David W. 1980. *Pacific Coast Nudibranchs.* Sea Challengers: Los Osos, California. 112 pp.

Bromley, Joan E. C., and J. Sherman Bleakney. 1985. *Keys to the fauna and flora of Minas Basin.* Acadia University Institute, Wolfville, Nova Scotia. 366 pp.

Gosner, K. L. 1971. *Guide to identification of marine and estuarine invertebrates, Cape Hatteras to the Bay of Fundy.* Wiley-Inter-Science, New York. 693 pp.

Gosner, Kenneth. 1979. *A field guide to the Atlantic Seashore.* The Petersen Field Guide Series, Houghton Mifflin Co., Boston. 329 pp.

Moore, G. M. 1964. Phyllum Mollusca, shell-less Opisthobranchia. (in) *Keys to marine invertebrates of the Woods Hole Region.* Mar. Bio. Lab. Woods Hole. pp. 153–64.

Newell, G. E., and R. C. Newell. 1973. *Marine plankton.* Hutchinson Educational, London. 244 pp.

Picton, Bernard E., and Christine C. Morrow. 1994. *A field guide to the Nudibranchs of the British Isles.* Immel Publ., London. 143 pp. (A catalogue account of 108 British species with many superb colour photos, 24 of which are species found in Atlantic Canada. The Sacoglossa, however, are not included.)

Thompson, T. E. 1988. *Molluscs: Benthic opisthobranchs.* Synopses of the British Fauna (New Series) No. 8 (Second Edition). Linnean Society of London. E. J. Brill, Publ., Leiden, Netherlands. (This 356-page, soft-cover field guide is outrageously overpriced, and many of the black and white drawings are of shockingly poor quality. Try to find a copy of the 1976 edition.)

Thompson, T. E., and Gregory H. Brown. 1976. *British opisthobranch molluscs.* Synopses of the British Fauna (New Series) No. 8. Linnean Society of London, Academic Press, London. 203 pp.

Angel, Heather. 1972. *Nature photography, its art and techniques* . Fountain Press, London. 222 pp. (Emphasis is on macrophotography.)

Bleakney, J. S. 1969. A simplified vacuum apparatus for collecting small nudibranchs. *Veliger* 12(1): 142–3.

Bleakney, J. S. 1970. A compact aquarium unit for macrophotography. *Veliger* 14(2): 196–9.

Bleakney, J. S. 1970. A mesofaunal collecting list for SCUBA work in frigid water. *Veliger* 14(2): 212–213.

Bleakney, J. S. 1982. Preparation of radulae and penial styles for scanning electron microscopy using 0.5 N quaternary ammonium hydroxide. *Veliger* 24(3): 297–299.

Clark, Kerry B. 1971. The construction of a collecting device for small aquatic organisms and a method for rapid weighing of small invertebrates. *Veliger* 13(4): 364–367.

Appendices

Appendix I.
Indoor Macrophotography Apparatus

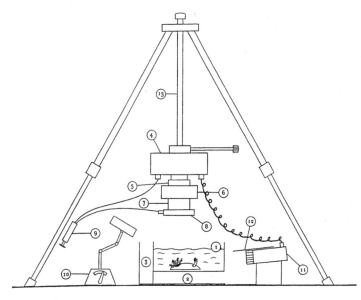

1.	Aquarium Chamber	8.	Automatic Extension Ring
2.	Background Chamber	9.	Double Cable Release
3.	Reflector Chamber	10.	Focusing Lamp
4.	Camera	11.	Flash Unit
5.	Extension Ring	12.	Glare Visor
6.	Variable Extension Tube	13.	Inverted Tripod Shaft
7.	Reversed Wide Angle Lens		

Diagram of a tabletop set up for macrophotography of animals in the 4 to 40 mm size range. The reversed wide angle lens increases depth of field at high magnifications and also increases working distance between lens and subject, thus elevating the optics well above the saltwater surface. A simpler system involves a macro lens with automatic extension rings and a single, not double, cable release. By gripping the feet of two of the tripod legs, while holding the

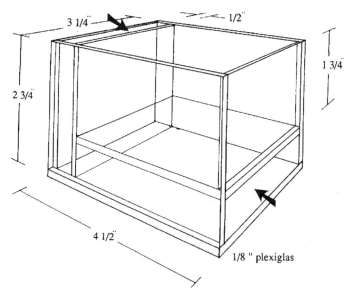

Labels on diagram: 3 1/4", 1/2", 1 3/4, 2 3/4", 4 1/2", 1/8 " plexiglas

Aquarium unit with a ventral pocket for insertion of background colours, and a vertical pocket to house flash reflectors

cable release in one hand, and looking through the viewfinder, you can focus and follow a live sea slug by sliding the two legs closer together, farther apart, or in unison. When you have something worth recording, trigger the camera and flash and capture it in colour.

The photo aquarium tank may be constructed of glass (for indoors) or plexiglas (for outdoors) or combinations of both. The practical approach is to make two each of three different sizes. Use clean, filtered seawater to avoid that snow storm effect in your photos from reflection of the flash off plankton and other drifting particles. Shoot the flash through the water from one side (thereby avoiding surface reflections) and bounce it back into the specimen's shadow with a reflector. The reflector can be grey, white, or aluminum foil. The background beneath the water tank can be dramatic black velvet or a colour and texture of choice.

In order to set up and get clicking as quickly as possible, while your specimens are still healthy and active, you should generate a reference table such as the example on the opposite page, but based on your own choice of camera, lenses, and film. With this information on a file card, you simply measure the sea slug, choose a slightly large field size, put on the designate lens and rings and set them the appropriate working distance above the floor of the aquarium. Add your specimen, look through the viewfinder, and all should be easily framed and focused by sliding the tripod feet slightly.

Exposure is controlled by moving the flash closer or farther from the tank. White specimens require less light as do larger animals, so you should deter-mine the appropriate flash distances and record them in a table on the other side of your file card. To obtain those really spectacular photos, the sea slug in your photo tank must be fully expanded. At the slightest disturbance or chemical irritation it may contract or even contort. Don't bang the table and don't let the water heat up. Don't contaminate the tank with soaps or with preserved specimens photographed previously. Don't use contaminated forceps; in fact wipe your forceps after each transfer of live specimens in or out of the aquarium. Wipe out the tank before a different species is introduced because mucous trails and defensive exudates left by the previous species usually irritate other species. An alternative method is to hold each species in the refrigerator in a separate little tank or glass dish. Each little aquarium can then be transferred directly to a photo platform with background and reflector chambers. This later unit is simply the aquarium photo tank without three of the water tank walls.

Example of Quick Reference Data Table for Setting Up Macrophotography Lenses and Flash

1. Pentax 50 mm lens & rings

Extension Ring No.	Work Distance	Field Width
1	200 mm	100 mm
2	150 mm	72 mm
3	100 mm	44 mm
1,2,3	75 mm	28 mm

2. Pentax & reversed wide angle lens (28 mm) & rings

Extension Ring No.	Work Distance	Field Width	Length of Slug
W/A lens	50 mm	20 mm	13–17 mm
W/A 2	45 mm	15 mm	10–12 mm
W/A 1,2,3	40 mm	10 mm	7–9 mm
W/A 3,3,2,2	30 mm	8 mm	5–7 mm
W/A 3,3,2,2,1,	130 mm	7 mm	3–5 mm

3. Flash distance from tank wall (in cm)

BRAUN 260 FLASH, KODACHROME ASA 64, 1/125, F/22.

	Basic Colour of Sea Slug		
Field Width	Purple/ Brown	Red/ Green	Yellow/ White
7 mm	0	0	1
10 mm	1	2	3
20 mm	2	3-4	5-6
44 mm	4-5	5-6	7-8

Appendix 2.
Annotated Classification Scheme for Sea Slugs

To put all the biological diversity into perspective, and into proper scientific terminology, there are within the phylum Mollusca (*moll* = "soft body") three major groups of snails within the class Gastropoda (*gastro* = "belly"; *poda* = "foot, walk"). Note that a direct translation of these Greek terms tells us that snails are "soft-bodied creatures that hoof it along on their bellies." Within that simple description is hidden the following classification complex, an organizational scheme that must constantly be readjusted as new information is revealed through both research and natural history observations.

PHYLUM: Mollusca. About 80,000 species.

CLASS: Gastropoda. About 40,000 species.

*Subclass 1. Prosobranch. Marine snails with spiral shell, operculum valve; gills in mantle cavity at front of animal (*proso = "in front"; branch = "gill"*); separate sexes; swimming larvae called veligers hatch from eggs.*

*Subclass 2. Pulmonata. Freshwater and terrestrial snails and slugs; spiral shell thin, reduced, or absent; operculum absent; gills replaced by a lung sac (*pulmonata = "lung"*); each animal is both male and female (hermaphroditic); without a larval stage, and the young hatch directly from eggs.*

*Subclass 3. Opisthobranchia. Marine snails usually with reduced or no shell; secondarily derived gills, eyes, and tentacles; mantle cavity and gills not in front but to side or to rear (*opistho = "towards the rear"; branch = "gills"*); hermaphroditic; usually a shelled veliger larva stage, but a few exhibit direct development from large yolky eggs. About 3,000 species.*

Thus, our little sea slugs are referred to by scientists as opisthobranch gastropod molluscs. Now we shall go one step farther and divide them into two interesting natural groups: the carnivorous order Nudibranchiata (*nude* = "naked"; *branch* = "gills"; meaning exposed gills not hidden in a mantle chamber) and the herbivorous order Sacoglossa (*saco* = "sac, purse"; *glossa* = "tongue"). This latter group are so named because instead of spitting out the discarded teeth from their rasping tongue surface as do all other snails, they save all the old worn teeth in a special throat sac called the ascus, an as yet inexplicable act. At this stage in your education you may, if you wish, chuck the derogatory term "slug" and refer to the creatures in question as either "nudibranchs" or "sacoglossans."

Within the Opisthobranchia are nine orders with their own suborders and families, to which the sea slugs of Atlantic Canada can be assigned. To better understand these groups and to more fully appreciate these unusual animals, learning some basic anatomy is in order. Figures in the Glossary (p. 7-18) depict anatomical features of representatives of the major types of local nudibranchs and sacoglossans. The following list outlines orders and suborders, but only those marked with an asterisk (*) have species included in this book. The other orders of opisthobranchs have yet to be studied in Atlantic Canada. Note that major food categories are mentioned for each group, because there is predatory specialization at these ordinal and subordinal levels, which is quite unusual.

Subclass: Opisthobranchia. *The sea slugs, which show a progressive loss of shell, mantle cavity, and gills and a consequent trend towards bilateral (not* *spiral) symmetry. The eyes are greatly reduced and not on tentacles, and gonads produce eggs and sperms simultaneously. About 3,000 species.*

Order 1. *Bullomorpha. Bubble shells, mostly burrowers in soft substrates.*

Order 2. *Pyramidellomorpha. Snail-like ectoparasites of polychaetes and molluscs, possessing a long piercing proboscis without radula.*

*Order 3. *Thecosomata. Shelled pteropods or "butterflies of the sea," feeding on phytoplankton. The foot is expanded as two wings, which are used for swimming.*

*Order 4. *Gymnosomata. Shell-less pteropods feeding on the above thecosomes, which they seize by means of tentacles, which in some species are armed with octopus-like suckers.*

Order 5. *Aplysiomorpha. Sea hares, having large tentacles that resemble rabbit ears; the shell is internal or absent. Length to over 90 cm and weights to 14 kg. Major herbivores of green algae.*

Order 6. *Pleurobranchomorpha. Diverse group, with and without shells, with a series of gills along the right side of the body. They prey upon sponges and ascidians.*

Order 7. *Acochlidiacea. Minute slugs living in the interstices of fine sands and gravels. Part of the "interstitial" fauna and poorly known.*

*Order 8. *Sacoglossa (= Ascoglossa). Algal sap-suckers; several have the ability to incorporate functional chloroplasts in their tissues and thus become photosynthetic snails. Body structure is the most varied of any group—smooth, papillose, leaf-like, no shell, univalve, bivalve, or even no heart. Old worn radular teeth are saved in a special sac, the ascus. When present, rhinophore tentacles are in-rolled, not flat or solid as in other Orders.*

Suborder 1. *Juliacea. Partially enclosed between two clam-like valves.*

Suborder 2. *Oxynoacea. Possessing a thin bubble-like shell, partially covered by lateral parapodial folds.*

*Suborder 3. *Elysiacea. Without a shell, great diversity of body form: simple smooth cylinder; leaf-like; frilly mantle ridges; or possessing cerata.*

*Order 9. *Nudibranchia*. The largest and most varied order, all carnivorous and attacking every kind of epifaunal animal and many planktonic pelagic animals as well. They are virtually immune from fish predation due to acidic and toxic defensive secretions, as well as stinging nematocysts derived from tissues of their cnidarian prey.*

*Suborder 1. *Dendronotacea. 10 families. With a dorsolateral ridge on each side of the body bearing a row of arborescent processes. Long rhinophoral sheaths distinguish this group. Most feed on cnidarians, but two genera,* Tethys *and* Melibe, *have expanded buccal hoods for scooping up swarms of small crustaceans.*

*Suborder 2. *Doridacea. 25 families. Mostly flat with a mid-dorsal anus surrounded by a circle of gills. Gills and rhinophores usually retractile into sheaths or pits. Feed primarily on sponges and bryozoans, but some species attack barnacles, compound tunicates, and tube-dwelling polychaetes.*

Suborder 3. *Arminacea. 9 families. Group of "different" slugs that do not fit neatly into any other suborders. Feed on cnidarians, bryozoans, shelled molluscs, and many bottom-dwelling (benthic) invertebrates.*

*Suborder 4. *Aeolidacea. 20 families. Group of delicate, beautifully formed and patterned species, all of which have rows or clusters of finger-like projections (cerata) on the dorsum. Rhinophores are not retractile. Cerata contain branches of the digestive gland and often store stinging nematocysts taken from their cnidarian prey (jellyfish, anemones, hydroids) in special cnidosacs. Also prey upon gooseneck barnacles, mollusc and fish eggs, and, uniquely, the Pacific genus* Phidiana *preys upon other sea slugs.*

ATLANTIC CANADA AND
GULF OF MAINE OPISTHOBRANCHS

(Tally so far is 24 genera and 47 species)

PHYLUM: *Mollusca*
CLASS: *Gastropoda*
SUBCLASS: *Opisthobranchia*

ORDER *Bullomorpha*
*Occur in the silts and muds of Atlantic Canada but
essentially unstudied.*

ORDER *Thecosomata*
Family *Limacinidae*
Limacina retroversa *(Fleming, 1823)*
Limacina helicina *(Phipps, 1774)*

ORDER *Gymnosomata*
Family *Clionidae*
Clione limacina *(Phipps, 1774)*

ORDER *Aplysiomorpha*
Family *Aplysiidae*
Not reported north of Cape Cod

ORDER *Pleurobranchomorpha*
Occur here but unstudied.

ORDER *Sacoglossa (= Ascoglossa)*
Family *Stiligeridae*
Alderia modesta *(Loven, 1844)*
Placida dendritica *(Alder & Hancock, 1843)*
Ercolania fuscata *(Gould, 1870)*
Family *Elysiidae*
Elysia chlorotica *(Gould, 1870)*
Elysia catula *Gould, 1870*

ORDER *Nudibranchia*
Suborder *Doridacea*
Family *Goniodorididae*
Ancula gibbosa *(Risso, 1818)*
Okenia ascidicola *M. P. Morse, 1972*
Family *Onchidorididae*
Acanthodoris pilosa *(Abilgaard in Müller, 1789)*
Acanthodoris subquadrata *(Alder and Hancock, 1845)*
Adalaria proxima *(Alder and Hancock, 1854)*
Onchidoris muricata *(Müller, 1776)*
Onchidoris bilamellata *(Linnaeus, 1767)*
Family *Triophidae*
Issena pacifica *(Bergh, 1894)*
Family *Polyceridae*
Palio dubia *M. Sars, 1829*
Palio nothus *(Johnston, 1838)*
Family *Cadlinidae*
Cadlina laevis *(Linnaeus, 1767)*
Cadlina marginata *MacFarland, 1905*

Suborder *Dendronotacea*
Family *Dendronotidae*
Dendronotus frondosus *(Ascanius, 1774)*
Dendronotus dalli *Bergh, 1879*
Family *Dotoidae*
Doto onusta *Hesse, 1872*
Doto "coronata" (Gmelin, 1791)
Doto *sp. (species A, Plate 13, Just and Edmunds, 1985)*
Doto *sp. (undescribed species)*
Doto *sp. (undescribed white species)*

Suborder *Arminacea*
Occur here but unstudied.

Suborder *Aeolidacea*
Family *Coryphellidae (= Flabellinidae)*
Coryphella verrucosa *(Sars, 1829)*
Coryphella gracilis *(Alder and Hancock, 1844)*
Coryphella pellucida *(Alder and Hancock, 1843)*
Coryphella salmonacea *(Couthouy, 1838)*

Coryphella nobilis *Verrill, 1880*
Coryphella *sp. (undescribed species)*
Family *Eubranchidae*
Eubranchus exiguus *(Alder and Hancock, 1848)*
Eubranchus pallidus *(Alder and Hancock, 1842)*
Eubranchus tricolor *Forbes, 1838*
Eubranchus olivaceus *(O'Donoghue, 1922)*
Family *Cuthonidae (= Tergipedidae)*
Cuthona gymnota *(Couthouy, 1838)*
Cuthona concinna *(Alder and Hancock, 1843)*
Cuthona pustulata *(Alder and Hancock, 1854)*
Cuthona nana *(Alder and Hancock, 1842)*
Cuthona viridis *(Forbes, 1840)*
Tenellia fuscata *Gould, 1870*
Tergipes tergipes *(Forskal, 1775)*
Family *Phidianidae (= Facelinidae)*
Cratena pilata *(Gould, 1870)*
Facelina bostoniensis *(Couthouy, 1838)*
Family *Aeolidiidae*
Aeolidia papillosa *(Linnaeus, 1761)*

Index